RUSSIA:
ABSENT AND PRESENT

LA RUSSIE ABSENTE ET PRÉSENTE is the first volume of the author's *European Triptych*; the other two volumes being:

STRUCTURE DE L'EUROPE
(*appearing shortly*)

and

VALEURS ANGLAISES
(*in course of preparation*)

RUSSIA:
ABSENT AND PRESENT

by
WLADIMIR WEIDLÉ

Translated by
A. GORDON SMITH

THE JOHN DAY COMPANY
NEW YORK

COPYRIGHT : 1952
by the John Day Company

All rights reserved

This book, or parts thereof, must not be reproduced in any form without permission

PRINTED IN GREAT BRITAIN BY
FERNDALE BOOK COMPANY LTD.
FERNDALE, GLAMORGAN, AND
294, CITY ROAD, LONDON, E.C.1

CONTENTS

	PAGE
ON THE MARGIN OF THE WEST	1

I. ANCIENT RUSSIA — 15
HORIZONTAL CULTURE 16
THE SMALLNESS OF THE ÉLITE 20
THE STATE AS OPPRESSOR 23
THE CREATIVE FORCES 26
A PEOPLE BUT NO NATION 30

II. MODERN RUSSIA — 33
THE FIRST REVOLUTION 34
WHAT WAS GAINED 38
RUSSIA IN THE WEST 41
THE WEST IN RUSSIA 46
THE GREAT AGE 51

III. THE CRACK — 56
THE TRIUMPH OF PETERSBURG 56
THE REVENGE OF MOSCOW 60
THE COMING OF THE CLERKS 64
WORN-OUT SYMBOLS 70
THE REVOLUTION ON THE WAY 74

IV. INTERRUPTED RENEWAL — 80
THE ECLIPSE OF NIHILISM 81
THE TREASON OF THE CLERKS 84
THE SILVER AGE 87
THE LAST CONQUESTS 91
SIGNS AND PORTENTS 95

CONTENTS

	PAGE
V. THE THIRD RUSSIA	101
FROM STATE WITHOUT PEOPLE TO PEOPLE WITHOUT STATE	102
THE COLLAPSE OF THE EMPIRE	106
THE REVOLUTION ENTHRONED	112
THE EURASIAN EMPIRE	117
ANTI-CULTURE	122
VI. THE RUSSIAN SOUL	129
THE FAMILY CONNECTION	130
FEAR OF LAW	135
HATRED OF FORMS	138
THE SPIRIT OF HUMILITY	142
THE FATAL ANTITHESIS	148

ON THE MARGIN OF THE WEST

EVERYTHING Russian, till not so long ago, appeared strange and exotic to the people of the West, if not wholly incomprehensible. It was so when Russia first thrust herself on the attention of the rest of Christendom, and the position had hardly altered, two centuries later, when Russian literature first burst upon the West and the arts of Russia began to be appreciated abroad: her music, her ballet and her theatre. Even then people were mostly attracted by these novelties because they saw in them something unusual and strange. It was only very lately that this state of mind seemed about to disappear, thanks to the interest that Russia is arousing to-day, and thanks to the greater receptivity kindled in the West by the successive catastrophes of the last thirty years. Western artists and men of letters are learning more and more to consider Russian culture as belonging to the common patrimony, as being an integral part of their European culture. They are acquiring, at the same time, a better understanding of some of the essential and irreducible differences. But in this double respect it is important to see Russia not only as she is, but as the centuries have made her.

. . .

The Russians themselves, like western historians, have often asked themselves if Russia is really a European country with a European culture, or whether she is not, after all, an extra-European country, westernised in haste and to the detriment of her true values by the sovereign and arbitrary will of Peter the Great. For more than a century Russian intellectuals have been divided by this problem. The "westernisers" saw the salvation of their country in a complete and rapid assimilation of western culture; the "slavophils", on the other hand, believed Russia could only be truly herself by strengthening all that separated her from the West, by remaining loyal to the distinctive characteristics of her past and developing a culture that should be in direct opposition to the culture of the West. The struggle went on, between the rival camps, throughout the whole of the nineteenth century. It has not ended yet. Among the Russian émigrés, the theories of the "slavophils" have been adopted more uncompromisingly than ever by the "Eurasians". These regard Russia as a world apart, between Europe and Asia, destined to produce an autonomous culture apparently far more Asiatic than European. As against these, the westernisers—and still more their revolutionary heirs of the twentieth century—showed they were incapable of conceiving a national culture with any distinct personality of its own. Their tendency, all the time, was to represent Europe (or the West) simply as the cradle of a civilisation at once rationalist and universal, capable of flourishing indifferently in any part of the world. They constantly tended to forget its other aspect, which is that of a group of national cultures, the variety and even divergencies of which are so far from impairing the unity of the whole that they are actually cherished for what they are, and would never willingly be lost.

Deprived of its own characteristics, the national culture of Russia could never lay claim to a European rôle. It is to the credit of the slavophils that they realised this; but they have gone too far in their desire to stress the specific and particular: they have set too little store by essential unity and ignored the fact that Russia's links with the West have made her, for all her marked individuality, a part of the cultural unity of Europe. Above all—and this is truer of the "Eurasians" than of their predecessors of the last century—they have confined themselves solely to the contemplation of "origins" without allowing for the creative forces of history. Hence they have tended to underestimate, or at any rate misinterpret, the life of Russia during the last two centuries; and especially the nineteenth, which had a meaning for her totally different from what it had for the rest of Europe, marking out as it did, more clearly than ever, the essential lines of her destiny.

But the slavophils' mistake had another origin as well, the

same origin as that of their perennial antagonists. It lay in the very idea each had formed about the difference between Russia and the West. For the slavophils, what they called Europe was something not belonging to them, something they were bound to hold inferior to what they possessed themselves. For the other party, Russia was primarily conspicuous for what it lacked, the absence of which made it inadequately (at any rate as yet) European. Imitating the western despisers of Russia, they delighted to proclaim (as far as they might) that the Slavonic languages had no connection at all with the European family; that Orthodoxy was wholly exterior to Christendom. As for the slavophils, who went to equal extremes, instead of attacking the point at issue they made retreats according to plan, retiring first from the banks of the Neva to Moscow, and waiting for the day when the old capital itself, together with its "white walls", would (doubtless with good reason) be too contaminated with westernism, insufficiently oriental.

"Oriental", "the East"—they are both very vague terms. What they mean, more precisely, is Asiatic and Asia. All one need say, from the terminological point of view, is that Russian culture has developed in Europe, so there is really no reason to describe it as Asiatic. If it must be described as "eastern", the word must be used in a European sense. The only way these terms can be used with any exactness is to distinguish, in the first place, eastern Europe from western (or what we may call the West), and then to distinguish both from the East or Asia. These considerations may provide no answer to the question once asked: How can one be a Russian? They make it clear, however, that its meaning could hardly be that which anyone would imagine from reading the *Lettres persanes*. The strangeness of being a Russian would not amount to a mere exoticism, a complete separation from the traditions of Europe and European ways of life, but rather to the fact of belonging to Europe in a particular way, a way that is not that of the West itself and hard for the western mind to conceive. For it is obvious enough that the historic destinies of the Slav-Orthodox world were never those of the Roman-Germanic Europe. Their respective heritages at the outset were different: on the one hand Greece, very slightly Romanised; on the other, Greece through the medium of Rome. The thing to discover is whether this division amounts to an absolute schism, precluding all union; whether, in spite of their common Greek and Christian roots, the two civilisations are really two[1] and not one; whether there are really two Christendoms, and also two Europes, not only disunited but as strange one to the other as the Arabian world from the world of China. If the questions are asked thus —and it is hard to see how they could be asked in any other way—they can have, it would seem, only one possible answer.

. . .

All those whose thinking has tended to cleave Europe in two, whether the original slavophils or their original adversary Chaadayev, have always invoked in their support the central fact of Russian history, her Byzantine inheritance. But was not Byzantium European? Is not Byzantine culture, the educator of eastern Christendom, essentially a Hellenic-Christian culture? Surely its influence on the West in the Middle Ages, like the fruitful influence of the West in modern times on the Orthodox countries, bears witness to an essential kinship and signifies something completely different from such a phenomenon as the Hellenising of northern India after Alexander, or the Christianising of China, or the propagation of the doctrines of Aristotle by the Arabs.

It is true, from the geographical point of view, that the Byzantine State has the appearance of an empire three parts Asiatic. But it must not be forgotten that the culture of Ancient Greece flourished also in the cities of Asia Minor, that the origins of the Christian faith itself are neither in Athens nor in Rome, and that the greatest of the Fathers of the Western Church belongs to Europe only in the historian's eyes, whereas the geographer, if he were allowed a say in the matter, would be perfectly justified in assigning him to Africa. Europe was

[1] As Arnold Toynbee believes. In the second part of the *European Triptych* I shall attempt to explain how my views about this differ from those of this distinguished historian.

born, historically, three thousand years ago on the eastern shores of the Mediterranean; a thousand years later, Germany and the British Isles were still not yet (in this sense) Europe; and as for the countries of Scandinavia, these had to wait for another thousand years before they could truly become part of Europe. Byzantine culture, undoubtedly, presented far more eastern (namely Asiatic) features than the medieval culture of the West; but these belonged rather to the periphery than to the centre: they transformed its outward aspect but left its nature intact. Thus Byzantine art, certainly the most revealing manifestation of this culture, underwent in the course of its thousand-year existence a number of extra-European influences. But while gathering these influences it knew how to resist them; otherwise its own influence in Italy or the Slavonic countries would have been just as superficial as that of Arabic art in Europe beyond the Pyrenees. And if it is true that eastern influences played the predominant part in the actual formation of the Byzantine style, it was in the new fusion of these elements that the creative energy of Byzantium is most clearly seen, in their subordination to the Greek sense of proportion and to an intensely Christian spirituality.

It was due to this energy, far transcending the domain of art, that Byzantium became the educator of the peoples of eastern Europe. Admittedly, among the gifts she bestowed on them, some bore typical marks of the East; but most revealed the classical and Christian spirit, and it was of these alone that the impress was decisive. Therefore it was not through its Byzantine education that ancient Russia was banished from Europe; on the contrary it was this that made her part of Europe, for this education consisted chiefly in the transmission of certain values inherent in the Hellenic-Christian tradition. What separated Russia from the West was only the difference between Byzantine and Western Christendom, between the spirit of classical antiquity as transmitted by Byzantium and precisely the same spirit as inherited from Rome. Hence there was no reason at all why it should have been a final and complete separation. In the historical perspective of Europe it is impossible to separate Rome from Athens, or Athens from Rome, or either from

Jerusalem, to which they are bound irrevocably by the respective missions of Peter and Paul. But the inheritance of the Acropolis and the inheritance of Golgotha had also passed to Constantinople, the second Rome; therefore the legacy Constantinople transmitted to her own heirs could never be considered as anything distinct from that which was the most precious patrimony of Europe.

It was the ancient literary language of Russia—"Old Slav", or "Church Slavonic"—that contributed very greatly to the making of modern Russia; and this, in the formation of its words, as in its syntax and idiom, is nothing but a perfect replica of Greek. In this respect, though it owes nothing to direct descent, it is much nearer Greek than the romance languages, in their medieval form, are to Latin. The clerics of the West, even when they used Latin, had far less idea of the ancient sense of style than had (say) Cyril of Turov, the Russian preacher of the twelfth century. His prose, with its cadences and rhythms and figures of rhetoric, is a very successful copy of that of his models, the sacred orators of Byzantium; and these, in their turn, had never lost touch with the stylistic traditions of ancient Greece. Similarly an ikon of Andrei Rublev, in all the richness and amplitude of its design, is closer to the authentic Greek tradition of art than any Italian work of the same period—a retable, for instance, of Lorenzo Monaco, a fresco of Masaccio, or even the gracious paintings of the school of Siena. Nor is it any accident that all the Russian words denoting higher spiritual states—meditation, contrition, humility, aspiration after wisdom, charity and active benevolence—are an exact translation of the original Greek compounds; moreover they keep the distinctive mark of Greek ethical notions, namely the fusion of the ideas of the beautiful and the good.

In its deepest aspect, what this Byzantine education involved was that the Christianity which penetrated Russia was tinged with the ideas and feelings of classical Greece. The teaching of the Church had the effect of inculcating into the whole people certain elements that were to become as it were a second nature to it. The idea of moral beauty, as the Russian literature of the last century bears witness, acquired a general familiarity and popular acceptance. It can be proved by reading Tolstoy (say *Alyosha Gorchok*), or Turgenev (*Living Relics*), or Leskov; or again Dostoevski's *A Raw Youth*, in which the old man, Makar Ivanovitch, living in the odour of sanctity, has only one reproach that he levels against people: that of lacking serenity, the ability to attain to inner harmony and repose. On the other hand the Old Testament, that powerfully affected so many countries of the West where Protestantism triumphed, never exercised any profound influence in Russia. For this reason, perhaps, the religious feeling natural to the people of Russia might seem to justify Rozanov's remark: "Orthodoxy responds admirably to the needs of a soul in harmony with itself, but not to those of a soul disturbed." But if there was ever a cult of the harmonious soul, it was—whatever Nietzsche might say—in the Greece of antiquity. And if Greece was not essentially European, where, it may be asked, is Europe to be found?

. . .

Byzantium lends itself so ill to the rôle of an anti-Europe that the successors of the slavophils, the new contemners of European unity we have referred to above, prefer to cut the ties between Russia and the West by relying not on elements traceable to Constantinople but on those they associate with Mongol Asia and Turco-Tartary. The history of Russia is bound up, for them, with that of Eurasia, the intermediate territory between Asia and Europe, but with a European frontier far more rigid than its Asiatic. They have defined its distinctive features very shrewdly; it is perfectly correct that these geographical facts have assured, one might say, a permanent contact with Asia and conditioned, in some ways, the general course of Russian history. But the initial error of the "Eurasians" lies in their supposing this conditioning to be essential and decisive.

The weakness of their case can be shown by an analogy. If they talk of Eurasia when they mean Russia, we might say Eurafrica instead of Spain. Geologically the Iberian Peninsula is part of the African continent, from which it is divided by the Straits of Gibraltar far less effectively than it is divided from

France by the Pyrenees. The Iberians, its earliest inhabitants, were of African origin and akin to the Berbers. As for the "civilising mission" of Ghengis-Khan, from which Russia benefited by way of the Tartar invasion, the Eurasians, much as they admire him, have to admit that his mission, if that was what it can be called, was far less durable than that of the Omeyads, and also far more problematical. Are we to infer from this that Don Quixote and Sancho, the Cid and Don Juan, really belong to some African or Islamic East; or that Velasquez and Goya are not Europeans? The seven centuries of Arab culture had a far deeper effect than the two of the Golden Horde. The Spanish character, Spanish manners and arts, even the mystical nature of Spanish religious sentiment, show features far more oriental in character than anything in the ordinary life of the Russian people. But Cervantes was no more a Moor than Pushkin was a Mongol; and the barrier of the Pyrenees, though better fortified by nature, has no more prevented Spain from being incorporated into the culture of Europe than the Carpathians and the Pinsk marshes have prevented the same thing happening to Russia.

Their geographical situation has marked out for the Russian people the path of their expansion and the shape of their empire, but not the direction of their cultural development. The Eurasians have not succeeded in proving the contrary by their careful collecting of certain facts that are both curious in themselves and also significant. The non-European elements they have found in Russia belong not to her history itself but to its raw materials. The Russian language, considered as primary matter and an ethnical datum, shows certain analogies, in spite of its origin, to the languages of Turco-Tartary, at any rate in its morphological structure; but this same language, from the point of view of national culture—namely as a literary language—developed, as we have seen, entirely from Greek, to which there was added later the influence of the literary languages of western Europe. Similarly, if there are Asiatic features in Russia's popular music, her higher musical achievements developed from the Byzantine impulse entirely, during the first seven centuries, and in the course of the two following, under the inspiration of the West. The same might be said of the plastic arts, in which, moreover, from the point of view of primitive tendencies in decoration, the whole of northern Europe forms a single region with northern Asia and Eurasia, and with all the latter implies in the way of a Slav or non-Slav population. As for the Asiatic elements that appear occasionally throughout history in arts and manners, they were due to no more than fleeting influences: those that were felt, for instance, at the end of the Muscovite period, in the sixteenth century and at the opening of the seventeenth, when Moscow had entered into relations with Persia, as well as with India and China, and was more than ever remote from the culture of the West.

What it amounts to is that certain materials used for the building, and plenty of decorative detail, could never have come from Europe; but is this any reason why the building itself should be officially catalogued as an Asiatic monument? When an attempt is made to grasp the general tendencies of Russian culture during the first seven centuries of its history, it becomes obvious that where it parted from Byzantine tradition it was in the direction of the West, not of the East. In the Middle Ages, Russia was a country less separated from the rest of Europe than was the Byzantine Empire, and with a way of life less different than the Byzantine from the life of the West. Kiev is slightly east of Petersburg, yet the State of Kiev was a Scandinavian foundation, and its first Russian dynasty, in the eleventh and twelfth centuries, allied itself by marriage, and more than once, to the princely families of France and Germany; and ancient Russian law belongs to the family of the Salic and other "barbarian laws". Many tendencies of its social life are identical with those of the same period in the West; the only difference is that in Russia they were less fully developed, they remained less stable and had fewer potentialities. Later, when the Mongol invasion broke the links between the Russia of Kiev and the West, Russian life grew more particularised and less analogous to the western; this was all due, very often directly, to the influence of the Asiatic invader. Yet it is important to stress that even at that time certain lines of development continued to point towards the West.

St. Sergius of Radonezh, the most sublime religious figure in medieval Russia, has a general resemblance to St. Francis of Assisi perhaps more than he has to the Byzantine saints; and even the schismatics of the seventeenth century, in spite of the contrast between their movement and the western Reformation, have certain affinities in the way of religious sociology to the Protestants, and especially the Puritans, of the West. In the representational arts the Byzantine tradition was faithfully maintained to the end; but in architecture and decoration, wherever they were less closely related to worship and ritual, forms were created that had no longer anything to do with Byzantium but were inwardly akin to the medieval art of the north and west of Europe. In the architecture of the sixteenth century, though it is impossible to trace direct borrowing from the West, there are manifest tendencies towards a soaring style reminiscent, to some extent, of that embodied in the Gothic. Taken altogether, the culture of ancient Russia might be said to be more western than the Byzantine; certainly it was wholly to the west of the Eurasian area that several of its principal centres developed. In the national life of Russia the regions of Novgorod and Pskov had a significance very different from those of Ufa or Kazan; and Moscow itself, after all, is far less remote from Vienna and Paris than from the cultural centres of India or China.

· · ·

Geographical and ethnological determinism is a tenacious error; but it is luckily one that it is easy to combat with a *reductio ad absurdum*. A people's history is not to be deduced from its origins, or from the primitive circumstances in which it was moulded. The future of a culture is not bound up for good with the destiny of the people that gave it birth. Should we deny to the Hungarians, on account of their origin, the right to count among the peoples of Europe? Are we to say the Jews alone were equal to constructing a Christian civilisation?

ON THE MARGIN OF THE WEST

Neither the geographical fact that the term Eurasia indicates, nor the cultural fact that we call Byzantium, has determined the future of the Russian people for ever. The true forces at work, in the history of the world and of Russia, will be estimated more justly by saying that there were certain initial data that set her a problem: it was a problem of which at first she was naturally unconscious, but it was one that throughout the ages she has sought to resolve, though it remains to this day not yet *decisively* resolved.

The initial data were the baptism of Russia and the cultural tradition of Greece and Christianity that she received by way of Constantinople. It was something the Russian people were perfectly free to reject; but if they declined to do so they had to make themselves somehow a European nation, to become an organic part of Christendom, the heirs of primitive Christianity and classical antiquity. Here, we venture to suggest, is the essential task that history set Russia, and it was a task she must have assumed with plenty of good will for we have seen her resisting forces, often considerable, that tended to draw her in the contrary direction. Even after succumbing to the Tartar invasion, she preserved her soul and never allowed herself to be tartarised. Yet the task was hard, for Asia had drawn close and the West was far off. Then the time came when Byzantium itself was only a memory, and one that released little vital energy. It was just this contrast, between Muscovite Russia no longer looking to the West, exiled in Eurasia, living more entirely than ever on her old patrimony, and that which the Tsar Peter so boldly conceived, a Russia resembling the West, a West in which all he could see was industry, applied science and technical progress—it was this momentous contrast that was later to seize on the imaginations of all, obscuring what was legitimate in the Petrine reforms and also the fact that without them (and before them) Russia was never wholly excluded from Europe.

The situation of Russia on the margin of the West was never any reason why she should have found herself outside Europe; but a too lengthy and too marked separation from western life involved considerable danger of her losing her way. Reunion

with Europe, a reintegration of Russia in the European group
of nations, became a necessary task that resulted finally, in
spite of the regrettable brutality that marked its early stages, in
assuring that the genius of the Russian nation should take its
part in the common task of Europe. If it was natural enough to
contrast *en bloc* the European West with Muscovite Russia,
there would seem to be rather less reason for contrasting it
with the Russia of St. Petersburg. In some respects, certainly,
the contrast was still justifiable, even two hundred years after
the death of the great Tsar; but far less so than before. Moreover a new situation had long since developed, completely
obliterating the old: Russia was becoming comparable to any
other European nation and could be contrasted with any one
of them, as it is legitimate to stress the contrast between
England and Italy, or between France and Germany. Apart
from these differences and contrasts Europe has no existence;
her unity, without them, would be reduced to a very poor
unison. Russia's problem was just this: to join in the choir,
not intoning the same note but making its own part heard.
The westernisers wholly misconceived the problem. They
regarded their country simply as a field for experiment, presented to western civilisation as a *tabula rasa*, with no culture of
her own nor any claim to belong to Europe in her own right.
All she had to do was to be *civilised* by the West, which from the
cultural point of view meant to them being colonised. Russia,
in their eyes, was first and foremost a "backward" country:
she had to "catch up" on the lead taken by the countries of the
West at her expense. What they failed to realise was that
Russia's being part of Europe never involved her resembling
Europe so closely as no longer to bear any resemblance to
herself.

It was only in the bosom of the European community that
Russia became fully herself. Her union with the West, far
from prejudicing the development of her own national destiny
(as the slavophils wrongly feared) was precisely what made
that development possible. One example, which is enough to
prove it, is that of Russian prosody. This, originally, had
counted only the number of tonic accents in the line; popular

poetry adapted itself to the system remarkably well, but a poetry other than popular was something that ancient Russia had never been able to create. At the beginning of the seventeenth century a written poetry began to appear, modelled on Polish poetry, in syllabic verse; but the structure of the Russian language proved refractory and the system was abandoned by the middle of the next century. Then Trediakovski and Lomonossov introduced the syllabotonic line, counting the number of syllables and tonic accents as well. This metre, not very different from the English or German, is that of all the great Russian poetry. Without being a close copy of any foreign system, it is certainly not a return to the old popular usage. The new verse of Russia, like the whole of her civilisation in this century and the next, was neither the old Russia alone nor the unadulterated West; it was rather the fruit of their mutual impact and alliance; it was Russia in her rightful place among the nations of Europe.

·   ·   ·

It is the business of the historian to concern himself with culture as it is that of the judge to concern himself with law. In the following pages this precept of Hegel's will be followed unreservedly. A tree is judged by its fruits, men or peoples by their works—which include a great deal more than the production of material objects. Moreover, judgment of interest is subordinate to judgments of value: if Russia's past or future is worth examining at all it is because there exists such a thing as a Russian culture. Now this culture exists only by way of Europe; it exists with Europe and in Europe. This is evident enough if we take a sufficiently broad view of the idea of Europe and fully understand its essential content. The West and Russia are like a tree with a double stem, with roots intermingling and branches constantly becoming more intertwined. But that part of the tree which faces the steppes has long been exposed to the winds of Asia, which is the reason why it has never produced so many leaves; many of its branches, too, are dead, and on a number of occasions the trunk itself has nearly snapped. It is her very *being* that appears to be Russia's age-long problem. A little while ago it might have seemed that this problem was about to be resolved; but the mighty tempest of thirty years ago has had the effect of raising it again in an entirely new form, and it is still not possible to foresee what the new solution will be. Nothing is certain, except that this time it involves far more than Russia herself.

In the spiritual world, Russia is on the margin of the West; in the material world it is the West that is on the margin of Eurasia. To-day this position on the map takes on a new historical significance. Pecherin, a Russian émigré who found refuge in England and remembered his Tocqueville, wrote: "Russia, with the United States, is entering upon a new cycle of history." This was in 1869. The prophecy is now in the act of being fulfilled, and the cycle that is beginning is raising the question of Europe once again. On what America and Russia can make of Europe's civilisation depends their future in the world of the spirit. But there is another future as well that depends on the same thing, and it is one that we may well think even more important, it is the future of this civilisation in men's hearts.

I

ANCIENT RUSSIA

RUSSIA's history is not one of success. She has not produced, whatever may happen in the future, a culture so complete, so stable and unified, as the cultures of France or England or Italy. Russian culture has lacked, if not coherence, continuity; it has the unity that belongs to the products of the same soil, but not the more complex unity that comes from an inheritance steadily cultivated and enriched, from generation to generation and from age to age. It is not that creative forces have been lacking, but the necessary condition for their full development was never realised till a century, or a century and a half, before that internal collapse which was greater than any that had yet befallen a European nation. Not only so, but there had been a series of what might be called premonitions of that collapse: the shipwreck of the Russia of Kiev, the downfall of the north-western republics, the political disintegration at "the time of the troubles", and (most important of all) the reforms of Peter the Great. The very migrations of her capital were bound to look strange when viewed from Rome or London or Paris, and the rupture that took place, between the last two centuries of her history and the first seven, was a wound not completely healed even on the eve of the revolution. Russia's historical growth has been interrupted more than once by profound upheavals, after each of which she had to re-educate herself and rebuild her political framework. This was all the more difficult in that the people as a whole remained largely indifferent to the task that should have been its own. The whole people of France, of England or Italy, took part in the major events of the West: in the Renaissance and *Risorgimento*, in the construction of the English State and British Empire, in the epic of the Crusades and the Revolution. But in Russia the people itself can never be seen in action, except in great inarticulate movements: the peasant colonisation, the growth of the Cossack community or sporadic risings against law and order, of which the last was the flight from the trenches in 1917–18. The principal difficulty that could never be surmounted—whether by the Russia of Kiev, the Muscovite Russia or the Russia of St. Petersburg—was precisely that non-participation of the people in the political and cultural life of the nation, its virtual refusal to provide the necessary labour for the establishment of a national tradition and continuity. The difficulty was present at the outset. It had to do with the very shape of the land itself.

HORIZONTAL CULTURE

If you ask an American what attracts him in the old world, his usual reply is its variety: the wealth of differences all concentrated in a confined space, so that there are incessant changes to be encountered with the minimum of travel. A Russian might say the same. Consider the contrast between regions as adjacent as Normandy and Brittany, Auvergne and Provence, Umbria and Tuscany. It is a contrast not merely in the aspect of their natural sites but in that of their towns and villages, their artistic monuments and their whole human atmosphere. There is nothing of the sort in the United States, where there are vast areas of the country, from east to west, without any remarkable alteration in scenery. Nor is there anything like it in Russia, where the whole country (apart from its late conquests in the South and in Asia) is simply a gigantic plain, furrowed by great rivers that in their wide slow course encounter few if any obstacles: a gently undulating plain that extends for thousands of miles, with its uniform fields and forests and villages and nothing to break the majestic monotony. There is beauty in this monotony, but it is a beauty wholly different from that of the West, which is a beauty strictly circumscribed, proud and jealous of its individual *otherness*.

Nothing suggests such a feeling of the infinite as this boundless extent of land; not even the sea, for a sea, and even an ocean, suggests the distant shores to which it gives access: shores that are an attraction to a Columbus or a Sindbad.

But the great plain, disappearing out of sight, has the air of leading nowhere; it prompts no enterprise, it suggests no thought but its own continuance for ever. A Russian might well admire the inexhaustible variety of the western countryside, that resourceful spirit which seems to be evinced by nature no less than man; but he will always feel himself cramped among its valleys and dales, he will find them too pigeonholed, too much divided and sub-divided with their disturbingly numerous railings and partitions, all those boundaries marked by hedges, all those ditches and barbed-wire fences. The aspect of his native land gives him a greater sense of freedom: not the freedom that consists in assertive action, the quest for fresh activities among distant peoples, but that other sort of freedom in which it is possible to get lost, to go away and forget all that is of yesterday and to-morrow, all that has to do with work and family and home. The word *prostor*, with its emotional colouring impossible to translate into a language of the West, expresses precisely that feeling of "free space", the feeling that rings so poignantly in the rambling nostalgia of popular songs, telling the anguish of being lost in the limitless plain where men are born and must eventually die.

Doubtless this is why nomads, and particularly the gipsies, have always exercised—in literature and poetry and music—so powerful an attraction on Russian sentiment. Not that the Russians themselves are a nomadic people. When they were in process of forming, the great Russian plain consisted of two separate zones very sharply differentiated: the steppes of the South and the forests of the North; and if this difference is less marked to-day than it was, it is due to the dogged and unceasing labour of the peasant. Yet the difference persists in a mitigated form, and the human type produced by the forests corresponds somewhat to that produced in other countries by mountains. This is all the more natural in that we have to do here with wild northern forests that had to be conquered by long and patient endeavour and also by an astonishing continuity of effort. The task was brought to a successful conclusion by the whole Russian people, in a vast work of colonising from the south-west to the north-east, from the steppe that begins at the gates of Kiev to the forests of Muscovy and of the Ural and finally those of Siberia. The constant background of Russian history, however little visible, is this slow-moving epic of the Russian peasant; it resulted in the subduing of the region of the steppes and that of the forests for the benefit of a vast intermediate area that has successfully been tamed by the harrow and the plough.

The Russian peasant, who accomplished this great work with the Ugro-Finish peasant (whom he peacefully assimilated on the way), gave proof of an uncommon energy and endurance. In view of an effort like this, it seems absurd to talk of "Slav passivity"; yet this overworked phrase is not without a basis of truth, if by passivity is meant not simply inertia—ridiculous to suggest in a case such as this—but a constant and unvarying activity and a certain reluctance to change direction. The great bulk of the Russian people, in the centuries during which their historic mission was accomplished, acquired a habit (that was certainly not laziness) of labouring to a rhythm they had adopted once and for all, a rhythm accepted by the individual as something obvious and necessary, more like a force of nature than an act of the human will. Hence, no doubt, come those impersonal turns of phrase so common in Russian. Nothing ever demands accomplishment; things are accomplished by themselves, not without human intervention but by means of actions constantly repeated, actions incapable of stopping, going on, one might almost think, spontaneously. So the Russian will say: "That has worked well", when any particular job has been finished satisfactorily: it is not the man who works, but the work itself that takes possession of the man.

Corresponding to this majestic uniformity of peasant labour —a sort of unmoving uniformity—there is an equally great stability in manners and customs, in culture and ways of life. The wealth of Russian folklore is vast; but, compared with the immensity of territory concerned, it has little variation. The differences, observable to-day between the North and the South, are due to the fact that the North has preserved more of the heritage common to both. The epics of the Kievan cycle, for instance, are known in our day only in the form they took in the far North, in the provinces of Olonetzk or Archangel; yet they celebrate the deeds of the Grand-Duke Vladimir, accomplished thousands of miles to the south. After remarking slight but inevitable local variation—due to differences of climate, of racial composition and miscellaneous influences—it may still be said that everywhere, in the north and south of the great plain as in east and west, the Russian people have always lived the same life, worked in the same fashion, and developed, after their conversion to the faith of the Eastern Church, the same beliefs and the same moral ideas. Russia has had a popular culture, both rich and homogeneous, a culture we here propose to describe as "horizontal". Their great difficulty has been to construct on this basis what may be called a high culture. Such a "vertical" culture—always complex and always more or less unstable—calls for the continuous efforts of generations on end; it can be built only on foundations very carefully laid and capable of resisting the test of centuries. For these foundations to be sound, the first essential is that they should not be too vast.

A horizontal culture is something to admire, but the place it can claim in the hierarchy of values can never be that of true works of art. Its normal function is to feed a vertical culture, by which it submits in return to be directed and transformed. All the best it produces rises to the level of true culture and so forms part of it, while the values of the latter in due course descend and are eventually disseminated among the people as a whole. The old popular art of the western peoples, after its fusion with the inheritance of antiquity, became the great Christian art of the western Middle Ages; on the other hand, the popular costumes of the French provinces recall nothing but the manorial fashions of the old régime, and the songs sung to-day in German villages come mostly from the almanacs of the eighteenth century. In Russia it was otherwise. The peasant never dressed up in the townsman's cast-offs, and before the revolution the romance of the book-stalls never ousted the ballad, which was something genuinely popular and often very ancient. The people assimilated, it is true, much of the old civilisation of the days before Peter, which was a feudal, municipal and monastic civilisation; but it was just this assimilation that hastened its decline and facilitated its destruction at the hands of the great Tsar—all the more so because, unlike the civilisation of the medieval West, it had never known how to use the creative energies of the people itself. So what happened in the end in Russia was that the people kept what they had been able to assimilate, used it for the benefit of their own popular culture, and left to others the task of building a higher culture, a culture based on a foreign model.

THE SMALLNESS OF THE ÉLITE

This problem of the two cultures, which remained till the revolution one of the most crucial in Russia, can be expressed equally well in quite other terms: those of the masses and the élite (or governing class). The élite in Russia, in every age, had been far too small compared with the mass of the population; it merged too easily into that mass; its creative work soon lost form and direction as it became adapted to cruder tastes and ideas. Moreover the very stability of the peasant culture meant that the recruitment of an élite was always difficult; which explains, of course, why the élite always contained so many non-Russian elements. This has never been contested in regard to modern Russia; but it was just the same (*pace* the slavophils) in ancient Russia as well. There was only this difference, that in the case of ancient Russia it was not a matter of various cultural élites, but only of a single political élite.

This odd state of affairs is as old as Russia herself. The earliest Russian State owes its existence, we know, to a group of Scandinavian warrior-merchants, the Varangians, known to the Greeks by that name of uncertain origin, *Rôs*, from which was later to be derived the words *Russian* and *Russia*. The first princes of the State so named bear very typical Scandinavian names and to their Slavonic subjects their Viking souls must have been mysterious indeed. From the foundation of the principality and the Kievan dynasty, the achievement of the Varangians was to initiate the people into an urban way of life, namely in the commercial cities along the famous river-route from the Baltic to Byzantium. They must have been slavonicised very quickly; but that does not alter the fact that it was not the Russians who created the core of a great and enduring State; they, at first, must have regarded their princes and their princes' retainers as foreigners, with customs they barely shared and a language that conveyed nothing to them.

Later, during the Muscovite period, the governing class again included foreigners—Lithuanians, Poles and Tartars— but its way of life and cultural traditions resembled more closely than before, and more closely than in the future, those of the mass of the Russian people. Yet it was not an organic emanation from the people; as a superstructure it was not built of the same materials as the foundation. It was always separated from the peasantry by its political ideas, by its methods of government and all its organising activities. From the reign of Ivan III and the capture by the Turks of Constantinople, the monarchical idea deriving from Byzantium took hold of the Grand-Dukes of Muscovy and their court. After the marriage of that prince to Sophia Paleologus, niece of the last Emperor, Moscow acquired the status of a third Rome, heir by divine right to the Eastern Empire. It was basing himself on this idea that Ivan the Terrible took the title of Tsar (Caesar), just as Peter the Great later (this time inspired by western examples) took the title of Emperor. Yet these ideas of Moscow as the third Rome, and the new national consciousness of which they are the highest but most bookish expression, hardly extended any further than clerical and court circles and the ranks of the nobility; the country districts knew nothing of such ideas, nor could they have found any use for them. To the people, the ponderous edifice of the Muscovite State was not quite so incomprehensible as was to be the westernised State of the last two centuries; but as they had not made it themselves they felt it to be something external to their own existence; they submitted to it, but still lived their peasant and patriarchal way of life.

This life could produce its own forms of social organisation, sometimes quite elaborate, but always primitive and rural, completely out of touch with what the State would have imposed, with its authoritarian and centralised methods. Hence the eternal difficulty of governing Russia and the drama inherent in her political history. Obviously the Russian people had to constitute itself as a State; it could never have remained content with the primitive forms of social organisation which were all that properly belonged to it; but it is equally evident that the State, knowing nothing of those forms or declining to utilise them, was bound to have recourse to innovations that were arbitrary and artificial. That is in fact what happened, so that there have always been two kinds of organisation in Russia; functioning one beside the other—or rather one above the other —with nothing to bring them together or cause them to converge to a common end. This lack of connection, of intermediate links, corresponds to an absence of hierarchical structure, one of the most striking features of Russian society. Between the scanty élite and the mass of the peasantry, wholly undifferentiated, there has never existed much in the way of intermediate bodies which could serve as a bridge between differing mentalities and give the nation effective awareness of common interests and common tastes.

The expression "social stratum" is more appropriate in connection with Russia than with any other European country. In the West, the active and creative part of a people can never be separated from the remainder, like cream from milk, for no one can say exactly where the cream comes to an end and the milk begins. Russia is alone in being like an enormous pancake; it is made of very good batter, but the jam that covers it has been applied too stingily. The horizontal culture flourished better in Russia because it was better preserved than in other countries of Europe; more than anywhere else, it penetrated the whole life of the people, giving it a meaning and justification that proved so satisfying that it needed to look no higher or deeper. Here, more than ever, the good was the enemy of the better; the success of a popular culture hindered the growth of anything more elaborate and hierarchical, that would have had to be based on some form or other of social inequality. This is what Russia has principally lacked. The State has always been a leveller: the great plain makes for equality, even if it be an equality of slavery. There was little corporate life; the free cities of Novgorod and Pskov were subjugated by Moscow; the State bore heavily on the people, and the people itself, no less equalitarian, always froze and neutralised any over-bold creativeness that appeared in its own ranks. A peasantry, it is true, is not a compact mass, like the inhabitants of modern cities and industrial agglomerations, and the population of Russia has never been dense; so it is a question here not so much of mass as extension, the effect of which is not stifling but rather dispersive and diluting. The Russian State, like Russian society and Russian culture, was always like something that had been built on shifting sand, subsiding every time before it was fully completed. History, according to Chesterton, is not so much a cemetery as a string of suburbs abandoned in course of construction. To no country's history is this so applicable as to Russia's: to her history in general and especially to her cultural history.

THE STATE AS OPPRESSOR

The State makes history, and to do so it must have a people. But what of the people themselves? Do they really aspire to a historical existence? In Russia, at all events, they seemed bent on showing they could well do without one. In their eyes, Rome was nothing; Byzantium itself more of a poem than an empire. Their own State seemed to them a pointless construction, a tiresome encroachment on the arable land. And who had been primarily concerned with building it? Foreigners. Western observers have always remarked how in Russia the governing class and the people seemed quite distinct. Thus the chronicler's famous account of the coming of the Varangians has a symbolical as well as a historical value. Russia has always been governed, its culture developed, by "Varangians", by strangers in spirit if not in race. It was Varangians who imposed on her the first *fiat* she ever knew; under Peter the Great, Varangians rebuilt her from the foundations up, and the revolution that set out to break and transform her once again was also the work of Varangians.

To meet its military, fiscal and administrative commitments, the old Russian State adopted primitive expedients that called for nothing but the simplest apparatus. These expedients correspond to two tendencies that are noticeable in the history of Muscovite Russia, from the fourteenth century till the seventeenth, and attained their final form, thanks to the reforms of Peter the Great, in the eighteenth: these were firstly the creation of a class of *State servants* (soldiers and officials) and secondly the attaching of the peasantry to the land, the ownership of which was vested in the same officials. By these means the State could assure itself of two things: human material always promptly at its disposal, and the maintenance of this material by peasant labour. In this way the soldier, the administrator and the judge, all necessary to the State, were fed by peasants established on their lands; with the peasant, for whose taxation the landowner could be responsible, the State was relieved of any concern. These methods, elaborated by the State in the course of centuries, explain the origin of Russian serfdom and the new Russian aristocracy, a privileged class with the sole right of owning serfs. The general system has often been compared with the feudalism of the West, but it differs from that in a number of respects, of which the decisive one is this: the feudal system, wholly conditioned as it was by its historical context, developed in a more or less spontaneous fashion. It was there, so to speak, before the State itself, and the latter could either participate in it or combat it. But the Russian system was due entirely to measures imposed by the State, all artificial and wholly utilitarian. Its influence was great, but there was nothing in it to provide any education, social and moral, or any personal differentiation, such as that effected by the feudalism of the West through institutions like chivalry, or common enterprises like the Crusades.

The reaction of the governed to these methods of government, always regarded as artificial and unfair, is a sufficient indication of the resentment they aroused. In a number of cases such reaction was flight. The steppes of the South were an excellent refuge for officials avoiding service, and also for serfs in revolt against serfdom. This was the origin of the Cossacks, free men organised in a kind of military community who warred for long periods against the Turks and the Poles. But there were other reactions as well, more violent in character, more menacing to established order and to the very existence of the State; meanwhile, on the part of the State, there were repeated attempts to enslave the people more directly and completely. The most famous of these attempts, before Peter the Great's, was that which gave importance to the reign of Ivan the Terrible. It was he who instituted a kind of State within a State by creating a wholly artificial élite, with no allegiance but to the person of the sovereign. This, as an instrument of coercion and surveillance, was perhaps as effective in his hands as, for the government of to-day, is the "apparatus" of a party, with its secret agents and corps of armed police. Yet with all his statesmanlike gifts and singular intelligence—and an irrepressible instinct for cruelty and tyranny—all Ivan himself could ever achieve in this direction was simply a reign of terror, that had the effect of disorganising rather than organising the country, and did much to bring about the general débacle that is known in Russian history as "the time of troubles".

These years (1603–13) revealed the latent anarchy that the Muscovite princes were powerless to exorcise. They provide the first examples of a truly popular movement, of what Pushkin was to call later "the absurd and pitiless Russian tumult". But the two classic examples of these great insurrections—without definite aim or even a vague programme, without intellectual backing and therefore doomed to failure—are those of the Cossack, Stepan Razin (quartered during the reign of Alexis in 1671), and that of Emelian Pugatchev (beheaded just over a century later in the reign of Catherine II). The two movements have much in common, which shows that there are constant features in Russian history and that its continuity was not broken completely by the Petrine reforms. Both began in the steppes of the South-East and on the Volga; the supporters of each were drawn from the Cossacks, fugitive serfs and deprived nobles; the social instincts that inspired both were the Cossack instincts of fraternity and equality and the peasant instinct of anarchy and revolt, challenging the oppressor-State and all its agents, the landed proprietors, officials and officers. The government quelled both revolts, though with a certain amount of difficulty; but Razin figures to this day in popular ballads and legends, and Joseph de Maistre was no bad prophet when he foresaw for Russia the possibility of a new revolt, this time successful and led to victory by a "university Pugatchev". At any rate the two leaders of these risings express in their own way, and with all the intensity of primitive instinct, the inarticulate hopes lying dormant in that other Russia: the Russia that the State could never get hold of, could never penetrate or assimilate to itself. That Russia evaded it, even when its submission seemed utterly abject: it would preserve its freedom, in the Russian sense, even if such freedom cost slavery to buy.

THE CREATIVE FORCES

For more than a century, Russian thinkers and historians of a certain school have been dismayed by the abyss between upper-class culture and the culture of the people, contrasting with this the harmonious unity, the ancient and autochthonous Orthodox culture, that preceded the reforms of Peter the Great. But that unity is an illusion. The abyss was enlarged by Peter's reforms, but it existed already. Popular Russia had always been an enormous plain; the stray hillocks of high culture that rose in isolation made very little difference to the appearance of the landscape. There existed, it is true, a tremendous unifying power: it was that of religion. But it is a mistake to think this could have sufficed for everything, or that in practice, as well as theory, Orthodoxy was always indivisible and integral. The Christian faith, as transmitted by the Eastern Church, impregnated deeply the whole Russian people; but it did so only by submitting to adaptation and transformation which gave it qualities not possessed in its original form. Peasant piety in Russia—the religious sentiment we see expressed in its customs and legends and popular hymns—was full of life down to the eve of the revolution. It was not only extremely beautiful in itself, but with its spirit of sacrifice and self-denial, its profound feeling of community in God, of human charity and brotherhood, we may well think it the loftiest form of popular religion and the most genuinely Christian that the world has ever known. Yet this kind of Christianity, compared with that of the Greek Fathers or of the great Doctors of the West, is bound to have the air of something stunted and impoverished, if not actually deformed, ignoring as it does so much of its sublimest potentialities. What is sufficient for the salvation of souls may be inadequate as a basis for a Christian culture.

Yet a culture existed, basically Christian and therefore akin to the medieval culture of the West; but it was a fragmentary existence, without fixed pattern or the national foundations needed for a complex and massive edifice. The Church was humble; for its greatest saints, charity was enough; they prayed in silence. Medieval Russia had never had a St. Bernard or a St. Thomas; it never had its *Divine Comedy* or its great cathedrals; it dispensed with great mystics, great theologians, great religious Orders. The subtlest and most perfect thing it produced, the spirit of its ikons, was also the most fragile. The loftiest forms of its religious life and thought were all inherited from Byzantium, and all the efforts of the best Russian clergy have always been directed to keeping these intact. Nor was there any desire among the people for change; yet, changes, just the same, were introduced surreptitiously. They were changes that made for disorder, dilution and ritualism, tending always in the popular direction, towards a piety ritualist in character and sentimental. In the end the Christian faith, like everything else, was itself absorbed into the vague meanderings of the horizontal culture.

The religious crisis of the seventeenth century reveals a curious state of affairs, almost the exact opposite of what we observe in the West at the time of the Reformation; for in Russia it was the head of the Church who desired to correct certain errors and put a stop to abuses, whereas it was the people who protested, appealing to venerable custom and the tradition of their ancestors. In the course of centuries, rites had been misinterpreted, errors had been creeping into the sacred books. The patriarch Nikon, a man of culture and ability, could not tolerate this corruption of the Greek inheritance and desired to return to the ancient purity; his opponents, on the other hand —among them the archpriest Avvakum, the one great writer of the age—desired, at all costs, to retain unchanged all the texts and rites then in use in the Russian church. So the schism that followed looks at first like a clash between two different shades of religious conservatism; but the real aim of the "old believers" (as the schismatics were later to be called) was really to defend the popular religion, and the thing they opposed was simply a more disciplined form of Orthodoxy, more learned and (if you will) more aristocratic. In the end it was the patriarch who won the day. It was a barren victory: the old Byzantine religious culture was already on the wane and the only result of the schism was to make permanent its rupture with the popular religion. But in spite of the rupture the latter was perpetuated, whereas the Greek inheritance grew desiccated and anæmic, to merge at last into the dead sea of popular devotion.

This, in general, was the fate of ancient Russia. Its creations, literary and artistic, had often been marked with grace and fervour, but they had always remained isolated, powerless to inaugurate any lasting tradition, therefore constantly in danger of losing completely whatever in their content was richest and most promising.

The most striking aspect of the literary patrimony of ancient Russia is its apparent poverty compared with the amazing wealth of Russian folklore; next to this is the fact that it never created a literary language comparable to modern Russian, or even to the *mittelhochdeutsch* or to the French of Chrestien and Joinville. Fundamentally, it was not so much a literature as a number of isolated works. Some of them are singularly beautiful, and these—it is significant—are in prose; for all the poetry produced by ancient Russia was orally transmitted and therefore forms part of the enormous mass of popular verse. From the purely artistic point of view, old Russian literature never produced anything finer than the famous *Gest of Prince Igor*, or more perfect than the sermons of Bishop Cyril of Turov, which belong to nearly the same period (the end of the twelfth century). In the five centuries that followed there was nothing to equal the refinement of diction, the suggestiveness of rhythm or the winning melody of Cyril's prose; nor did all this long period produce a poet with the genius of the unknown author of *Prince Igor*, whose skilfully rhythmic prose produces an effect as intense as that of verse itself, and is based on the subtlest melodic inspiration. Indeed, its unrivalled artistry has given birth to the theory (erroneous, in my opinion) that it is really a pre-romantic forgery. A single manuscript transmitted it, and this was destroyed in the fire of Moscow in 1812. Certainly, during the two next centuries there was only one imitation, and a very feeble one at that. So too in the other case: a language so astonishingly supple as that of Cyril, so conscious of artistic device, is never found again in the history of ancient Russia. In the sixteenth century, Ivan the Terrible, who had considerable literary gifts, used a strange, twisted and pedantic style, half-way between Russian and the Slavonic of the Church; whereas in the following century the archpriest Avvakum simply wrote as he would have spoken, thus creating his own unique and strictly oral style that derives its strength, its devastating emotional truth, precisely from this absence of any style at all.

The great century of old Russian painting was the fifteenth, the century in which literature showed few signs of life. At the beginning of it there appeared the masterpieces of the greatest Russian painter of all time, Andrei Rublev; and the end is marked by the wonderful frescos of Master Denis at the monastery of Therapont. There were works of hardly less value produced in the two preceding centuries, but in these the Russian contribution barely emerges from the obvious supremacy of the Byzantine. By the middle of the following century the decline had begun. So the dates we get here, far from corresponding to those of the literary masterpieces, are not even those—which is stranger still—of the greatest period of architectural development. And this development, considered by itself, is a striking reminder of the strange discontinuity to be observed in the cultural history of old Russia.

At the end of the twelfth century, and early in the thirteenth, an exquisite style in architecture flourished in the Duchy of

Vladimir-Suzdal; and another, less finished but with great delicacy of feeling, began to develop rather later in the Novgorod region and lasted for a hundred, even two hundred years. The two styles never converged, as happened (for instance) with the Romanesque architecture of Normandy and the Ile de France, both of which contributed to the formation of the Gothic. By contrast, in the neighbourhood of Moscow and in the capital itself, the sixteenth century produced an entirely new style, inspired, we may suppose, by the wooden architecture of northern Russia, and boldly breaking away from the example of Novgorod and Suzdal. This new style is certainly the most original that Russia ever produced, and the most spontaneously Russian; but its development was hampered by the ecclesiastical authorities and the few examples that survive are specimens rather of promise than of achievement. It is the same in the case of a very interesting group of Muscovite churches, dating from the extreme end of the seventeenth century; these, on the eve of the disappearance of the old Russia, show the tentative beginnings of yet another style, also based on wooden architecture but this time on that of the Ukraine. Masterpieces were produced by all four styles, but there was never anything in Russia like the fully-formed classical style in Italy or the Gothic in France; there was no creation, by the combined resources of the nation, of a common artistic language, capable of enduring because it answered to the profoundest needs of the national soul.

A PEOPLE BUT NO NATION

A nation is simply the spiritual body that a people acquires in the course of its history: it is a changing form that even while changing remains faithful to itself. Though it never lacked genius, though it was still less lacking in enduring patience, the Russian people, in the whole seven centuries of its ancient history, never once achieved this form or embodiment. Genuine efforts, even if spasmodic, were made by its all too scanty élite; but every single cultural achievement of that élite was squandered by the people as rapidly as it was annexed. There are examples both in literature and art: one has only to compare the monuments of the seventeenth century with those of the centuries that preceded it. What is noticeable at once is an ever greater proliferation of forms, all merging into the soft and vague and indecisive; a reducing of everything to the ornamental and decorative; an internal dissolution; a falling away in everything that suggested the distinctive or sublime. Not that the final result was unbeautiful, but it lay at an entirely different level; it had dropped a number of degrees in the hierarchy of human values. German students of folklore, describing what happens when a poem is transformed into a popular ballad, are fond of using the term *zersingen*. We might describe the whole culture of old Russia as *zersungen*: it had been transformed into folklore even before it was replaced with a new civilisation imported from the West. The ornamentally florid ikons and frescos of the seventeenth century, the architecture that was purely decorative and indifferent to considerations of space and construction, tales of adventure without style or profound interest—none of all this can be compared with Rublev's *Trinity*, with the churches of the twelfth or early sixteenth centuries, with the sermons of Cyril or the *Gest of Igor*. Russia's oral poetry and popular arts excel many others in wealth of forms and warmth of feeling; but they developed at the expense of great art and higher literary achievement, which they diluted down into vague meanderings and everlasting ornamentation.

What is true of its arts and literature is equally true of its civilisation as a whole. It was always tending to return to its starting-point: to sink back, so to speak, to the level of the horizontal. The great creative works of ancient Russia are like the temples of Indo-China, swallowed up by the virgin forest that surrounds them. Only here it is not a question of the tropical forest, aggressive and poisonous; it is only a plain, extending far beyond the limits of the horizon, and a people of peasants. These can tell stories and sing beautiful songs; they can build white, pathetic churches, at the edge of a wood, among their fields or beside rivers; they are a gifted people, skilful in all the manual arts, but completely indifferent to whatever may be done in Kiev, to the achievements of Moscow or Novgorod, content to adapt to their tastes what they appreciate and quietly leave all the rest alone.

For Russia the two last centuries of her history were a period no less glorious than tragic. But if the glory was something new the tragedy simply prolonged, in a different form, the tragedy of the seven preceding centuries. The Tsar Peter had not to destroy a healthy and fully developed national culture; that was in ruins long before Peter came to the throne. Numerous products of its decadence survived, to enrich the life of the peasants during these two latter centuries, when the peasantry was severed still more from any high culture; but it is impossible to claim that the old national culture was preserved intact. It was nationalist historians, led by Karamzin, who rediscovered the old Russia. The people themselves hardly thought of it; they remembered Razin, but they had forgotten his opponent, the "gentle" Tsar Alexis. From the Grand-Duke Vladimir, right down to Peter the Great, Russia's history had been full of movement; it had been rich in events and not without achievements; but the great problem of national existence was one that Russia herself had never been able to solve. The common life of a nation, that precedes—historically as well as logically—the appearance of what is known as a national consciousness, depends on popular participation, even though subtly graded, in the creation of the highest cultural values. The direct producer of these values is the individual, but the individual as a member of a group; and the group, either directly or through the medium of other groups, must itself be part of the life of the nation as a whole. It is this integration and this hierarchy that was lacking in ancient Russia, as they were to be lacking also in modern Russia. Hence its final disintegration into the formless, impersonal and wholly inarticulate, into the indefinite windings of the horizontal culture. And when all was tottering, effete and liquefied, there was obviously very little left to destroy.

II

MODERN RUSSIA

THE two centuries of the new Russia, inaugurated by the reign of Peter the Great, are as much a closed era to-day as the seven preceding centuries of the old. Lenin's new transfer of the capital to Moscow symbolised as neatly the end of an epoch as the founding of St. Petersburg—which relegated to the past the Russia of Tsar Alexis and the patriarch Nikon—indicated its beginning.

Consequently the historian's viewpoint is very different from what it was some thirty years ago. Standing outside the age, he is in a far better position to understand it. He can see its greatness and its drama—and the full extent of both. He can see that, in spite of its shorter duration, it counts for as much as the age that preceded it; indeed in some respects more, for its life was more intense, its tempo more rapid, its cultural values more numerous and varied. The eighteenth century was a period of growth and expansion, of vastly increased wealth, both material and spiritual; and it prepared the way for the next, Russia's "great century", without which, in spite of everything the old Russia may have produced, it is impossible to think of Russia as such, with her own characteristics among the other nations of Europe. Yet in the course of these two centuries, was there ever a moment when her balance was not endangered, when she could forget the revolution that Peter had effected, or was without a presentiment of the revolution that was to come—that which has created, in our day, yet another new Russia?

It would seem not. That is why the whole St. Petersburg epoch, and the city itself, appeared to many like a kind of spell or mirage, a long dream that anyone could foresee would one day vanish completely.

THE FIRST REVOLUTION

In the eyes of the slavophil historians of the last century, the changes imposed on Russia in the age of Peter the Great were a catastrophe without precedent; they broke the spirit of the country and they robbed it indefinitely of its free and natural development by thrusting upon it forms of life and culture that it was never capable of absorbing and transforming—at any rate in such a way as to make them fully its own. Now this idea was entirely erroneous. It ignored the European—even the western—characteristics that were already present in the old Russian culture, and thereby attributed to the helmsmanship of the great pilot an arbitrary element that never belonged to it. It was wrong, too, in that it took no account of the obvious analogies between this particular epoch of Russian history and the period when France, together with Germany and England, was in process of assimilating, more or less happily, the culture of the Italian Renaissance. But it rests, none the less, on a central intuition that is perfectly just. It was not a more or less radical reform that had occurred: it was a revolution, and therefore a catastrophe. But this was due to the Tsar's particular methods rather than to the general direction of his aims: not so much to the depth of the contrast between Russia and the West as to the quality of the western elements that happened to take his fancy and that he therefore felt bound to introduce into Russia.

There is a very close parallel to what happened in Russia during the reign of Peter and those of his immediate successors: it is the invasion, at the beginning of the modern era, of the Germanic countries (and specially Germany herself) by cultural patterns derived from the Latin countries: from sixteenth century Italy and seventeenth century France. This second Romanising of Europe, reaching countries that had never been touched by the first, explains very largely the unleashing of that Nordic reaction called the Reformation, and the strange paralysis that overtook art and letters in Germany soon after the deaths of Dürer and Luther. The crisis was serious and had many repercussions; German culture itself was within an ace of perishing, and for a long time the clash of the two worlds seemed irreconcilable. But in spite of everything it was reconciled at last in the great age of Germany, of which the beginning and end coincide very nearly with the birth and death of Goethe.

The two worlds that were in head-on collision in Russia might have been more violently opposed, even less reconcilable than the struggle in Germany (though there were obviously convergent developments on each side); but the fact remains that they too were reconciled, in the great period of Russia that extends from the birth of Pushkin to the death of Tolstoy. The only difference is that the German crisis was a more or less free and spontaneous war between two great historical forces. There was no exterior constraint that obliged Dürer (for instance) to follow Italian models, or Opitz, later, to adopt French versification; whereas western civilisation was imposed on Russia from above, by decree, and with the frantic intransigence of a very raw genius. Again, in Germany it was Titian (one might say) that confronted Grünewald, the spirit of Leonardo or Machiavelli confronted that which had once been the inspiration of Master Eckhart, and was in later days to inspire Jacob Boehme; but the culture of old Russia, declining and by this time largely disintegrated, received its death-blow in quite another way. It was swamped by a flood of third-rate prints and horrid little *trompe d'œil* paintings (the only kind of art that the Tsar understood); by two-headed embryos preserved in spirits and manuals of etiquette—deprecating, for instance, the practice of bowing in the presence of ladies through open windows, or, at a formal banquet, surrounding one's plate with a trellis-work of bones.

Such was the end of seven centuries of Russian life. It was not enough to banish and condemn them, to replace them (till something better served) with the merely shoddy; there had to be a deliberate effort to make them look abject and absurd. The Tsar himself cut off the patriarchal beards of his courtiers; he commanded all his subjects, except priests and peasants, to shave the chin and dress in the fashions of the West. Even customs that were purely domestic were abolished; others, such as the German Christmas tree, were made obligatory.

One of the Tsar's favourite amusements was staging indecent parodies of ecclesiastical processions. He took part in these himself, and his old tutor, Zotov, had to play his allotted part of "most-clownish and most inebriated Patriarch". It was not a transforming of the old civilisation of Russia by grafting on it forms purloined from the West; it was rather a matter of getting rid of it altogether as expeditiously as possible; and then, after thoroughly clearing the ground, building something that was perfectly regular and rational, something essentially useful, based on the cotton-mill or the barracks, reminiscent of the London Docks or the workshops of Saardam.

Peter was the first of all technocrats in history, and what are called his reforms are really the first revolution—in the full sense of the word—that Europe ever knew. The events in England during the preceding century never aimed at making a muscum-piece of the whole body of English tradition; and generally speaking, before 1789, no one had ever envisaged so complete a recasting of the established order; certainly no one had succeeded so quickly in manufacturing a thing that was hitherto unknown: an *ancien régime*. It is true that, like all revolutions, it stopped somewhat short of the end it was designed to achieve. Most of the links with the past were broken, but not all of them; Russia continued to develop in the direction laid down for her, but she did not become immediately what Peter wanted to make her. Everything negative, however, in the consequences of his reforms is simply due to their revolutionary character. Everything hard and artificial in the old Muscovite State, everything it had imposed from without on the national life, evolved more than ever towards arbitrary efficiency and bureaucratic automatism. The separation that existed already between peasant Russia on the one hand, and on the other those who governed it and produced the cultural values it never quite understood, became far more accentuated by the fact that henceforth these values had to be constructed of borrowed materials, to be assimilated only slowly by the mass of the people, even if they were capable of being assimilated at all. Finally, though everything the Tsar introduced into his country was no doubt perfectly rational and useful, it was also

—and this is what, perhaps, is most deplorable of all—quite soulless.

The element in the Petrine revolution that augured worst for the future of Russia can best be seen in the Tsar's religious policy: the abolition of the patriarchate, the reorganisation of the Church's administration on the Protestant model, and the founding of the "holy synod". The procurator-general of the synod, nominated by the sovereign, ruled the Orthodox Russian Church for the next two centuries; he was the principal instrument of its enslavement to the State and of the partial drying-up of its creative energies. The old Russian culture had been constantly nourished and sustained by its religious roots—these, at any rate, being the same for all. It was a culture that had very little practical use; in the way of organising ability and technical skill it was very ill-equipped for providing the State with what it wanted. But it was warmed with the inward fire of an intense religious feeling, and this remained to the end —in spite of excessive developments in ritual, particularly after the sixteenth century—the almost unique source of everything sublime or profound it was capable of creating. The new Russian culture, inaugurated by Peter the Great, was to lose the benefit of this unity and warmth, at any rate till the return, by the great geniuses of the next century, to the hidden sources of Christian inspiration. It never became, it is true, so purely utilitarian and technical—so American, as we should say today—as the reformer himself had wished; but as long as it remained in contact with the State—as long as it was centred in Petersburg—it continued to retain something that was official and formalist; and it was this that Moscow and the provinces resented, seeing in it something foreign to the mass of the people. To some extent at least the latter had preserved their folklore, their ancient horizontal culture. And they had their priests. These, at any rate, had never forsaken them; they were nearer to them than the governing classes, even in their physical appearance, since Peter had allowed them to retain their traditional habit and their long venerable beards. So the people kept back something for themselves that the élite were in danger of losing; but for a culture to endure, people and élite together must be capable of sharing its most intimate treasures.

WHAT WAS GAINED

Rather more than twenty years ago, there was discovered in Siberia a large Russian village in the forests of the far North that for two centuries at least had lost all contact with the rest of the country. The language and customs of the inhabitants, their clothes and the way they furnished their houses, corresponded exactly to the period of the Tsar Alexis. Here, as it were frozen, was an example of the old Russian folklore culture, such as it might very well have remained to this day but for the violent prod it received from the brutal genius of Peter the Great. The Tsar certainly provides us with our first authentic example of what a present-day historian[1] very happily labels: *Homo occidentalis mechanicus neobarbarus*. His horizon was limited; all he saw was the immediate, the applicable, the practical; but his instinct was far more penetrating than his thought, and while bungling many of the details he succeeded in the essential—like a surgeon with little consideration for his patient who is content with saving his life. The task he had set himself was to create a new Russia—by what means he could and with the materials he had to hand—which should take the place of the other Russia that was crumbling into ruins around his cradle. But he did more than this. He brought back Russia into Europe; and not only Russia but virtually the whole of Eastern Christendom. The founding of his new capital, St. Petersburg, corresponds to the founding of Constantinople, fourteen centuries before.

The fact that Russia was truly destined to be united to Europe, and that she was capable of profiting by it, is proved by the whole of her subsequent history. The narrow rigid framework, in which Peter intended to confine his country in order to control and guide it the better, burst asunder on the morrow of his death; thereafter, to avoid stifling the exuberant vitality of the nation, it rapidly expanded and grew supple.

[1] Arnold Toynbee.

After passing through a number of troubled periods, Russia attained at length, and happily enough, that necessary blend of order and disorder that alone can foster the normal development of a nation. "The Russian government," wrote Custine, "is an absolute monarchy tempered by assassination." This was an excellent definition of Russia's particular blend of order and disorder, where the principle of organisation was represented always by the absolute power of the State, and the principle of liberty by a condition of partial and intermittent anarchy.

All the same, the reigns of Elizabeth and Catherine II are a period that Russians have always remembered with tenderness, and also with not a little gratitude and pride. Peter the Great's fat and indolent daughter, who vowed on coming to the throne she would send no one to the scaffold and who (in spite of a few exhibitions of cruelty) actually kept her promise; the little German princess, charmingly intelligent, a little too up-to-date for the requirements of an anything but up-to-date people —these two governed an enormous empire and succeeded, not without glory, in enlarging it still further. Their success was due to the fact that they relied in their work on a young and vigorous ruling class. This owed to Peter, if not its original rise to power, its firm establishment and final shape. Together with the new capital, the nobility—this new élite, infinitely wider in its bounds, more active and more capable of surviving than the old—was the Tsar's best gift to the Russia of the future. In spite of Lomonossov and other parvenus of genius, what Russia produced down to the middle of the next century, in the way of great men or cultural values, all derived from this class, or could never have developed in any but the environment formed by this class. Moreover, not being exclusively hereditary, it was never a closed caste. Nobility was won by serving the State, either as an officer or civil servant; the fact of belonging to an old and aristocratic family, of being descended from a Riurik or a Gedimin, conferred no special privilege on those who could boast of it. Russia's cultural, political and social ascent, between Peter I and Alexander I, was wholly the work of this new nobility.

Even more important than the vast increase in the country's

material resources and her military conquests, than the feeling of power these awakened and of faith in the future, was what the eighteenth century contrived to accomplish in the nation's interior life. Under Catherine, Russia's literature, art and intellectual activities had no resemblance at all to the barbaric technolatry and Babylonian mixture of forms that were typical of the reign of Peter the Great. Russia's architects, her painters and sculptors, were beginning to collaborate with the great foreign artists now working in the country. And they were soon to rival them. Bazhenov, Chubin, Levitsky were all apprentices who turned masters. Music and the theatre were taking their first flights under Catherine; Derjavin, her minister and the official singer of her glory, is chronologically the first great poet of modern Russia; Karamzin, who was beginning to write in her reign, is the first great writer of prose. But the finest creative work of the time was not that of any isolated genius, it was a collective work in which all the writers and poets, all the men of letters and the "educated" of the period, collaborated according to their personal abilities: it was the creation of the literary language of Russia. The frightful jargon printed in the reign of Peter the Great became in less than a century one of the richest instruments of expression, and most supple, that a people's creative imagination ever devised. Elements derived from Old Russian, as it was spoken and written, from Church Slavonic and from the idioms of the West, all mingled together in a harmonious whole that was soon to attain perfection in the work of Pushkin. A creation such as this, so necessary and invaluable, old Russia had proved to be beyond her capacity.

The new culture, born of the Petrine revolution, had originally been no more than a heterogeneous mass of imported articles; but the new élite assimilated these so quickly that by the end of the eighteenth century a Russian culture had already come into being, one more homogeneous and more stable than the old. The culture was Russian in the strictest sense of the word, expressing states of the soul and creating truly Russian values; and if the people themselves only half understood it, it was not because this culture was insufficiently national, but because there was as yet no nation in existence to correspond to it. Peter the Great's "enlightened" (that is, ferociously rationalist) despotism, which regarded the state as a straitjacket with which to constrain a people always prone to unreason and ready to revolt, had done little to organise that people from within, to bring about the necessary inequalities and hierarchies that could ultimately initiate a national life. The carpenter-tsar was too busy knocking up his barrack to address himself to a trade that called for vastly more patience and leisure—that of a gardener. Russia is indebted to him both for all she created in the next two hundred years, and also for the immediate shipwreck of her culture. But at the close of the century that saw Petersburg born, and at the beginning of that which saw its highest splendour, the prestige of the new State and its new civilisation came almost to eliminate the memory of past troubles and disguise the symptoms of troubles to come.

RUSSIA IN THE WEST

One of the great events that determined the course of history in eighteenth century Europe was the transformation of Muscovy—a country inaccessible and exotic, more Asiatic than European, and politically concerned only with its immediate neighbours—into a powerful empire open to the West, adjoining it north and south, and possessed of a momentum that made its movements and future designs matters of very great interest to the whole of Christendom. The visits paid by the Tsar to Holland, London and Paris, have from this point of view a symbolical value: the Emperor in person presents the West with this new state of affairs, thus stressing (what was obvious in itself) the momentous effect of his victories and reforms. His personal prestige in the "enlightened" century is itself a phenomenon that deserves attention. To his contemporary, Daniel Defoe, he is the model of a "self-made man", a kingly Crusoe, whose isle is a vast empire in which he secures the triumph of civilisation by the means fortune offers him and by making a clean sweep of everything to do with the past. The "enlightened" sovereigns were to take him for their model, and his posthumous fame contributed not a little to the prestige of the new Russia, attracting a host of foreigners to this capital of his that his will had redeemed from the marshes, so that it became, what it was to remain for two centuries, a city essentially cosmopolitan.

Russia burst upon Europe, not only in war and commerce and international relations, but intellectually as well. From now on it became easy to gain fuller information of her than that contained in the letter of the poet George Turberville, English ambassador in Moscow in the reign of Queen Elizabeth, who thought it sufficient to note that the country was extremely cold and that its inhabitants were stamped with the marks of bestiality:

> *Lo thus I make an end: none other news to thee,*
> *But that the country is too cold, the people beastly be.*

And information, now, was generally more reliable than that available in previous centuries; though even to-day it is not uncommon for people in the West, well informed on the affairs of Europe and America, to entertain the absurdest ideas about Russia. But from the reign of Peter, if Russia was still a mysterious country, she was no longer a closed country. Those who came to see with their own eyes, and those who merely judged by hearsay, were all impressed by her vastness, by the richness (even though latent) of her soil, by her future possibilities, by the scale of her potentialities for good as well as for evil. Not least striking were the contrasts she offered: the pageantry of the capital and the extremely simple manners of the provinces; the young courtiers dressed out in the fashions of Versailles and the village priests, rustic and bearded. A new idea was gradually formed about Russia, naïve enough still—as is shown by the set of tapestries of Jean-Baptiste Leprince known as the *Jeux russiens*—but less bewildering than before, and certainly less forbidding. In the reign of Catherine II, who was at pains to impress the world that she was herself the fashionable ideal of a sovereign, the idea formed abroad of the resources of the country and the splendours of its court was still further enhanced, and to such an extent that other glories were eclipsed. The essential fact, historically speaking, is that it is impossible to imagine eighteenth century Europe without this "police empire", ruled by a sovereign who corresponded with the Encyclopedists.

But the country's prestige at this period, and later as well, was obviously not due to the new culture she had produced, of which so far very little was known outside Russia, but to her successes in diplomacy and on the field of battle. A steadily rising line can be traced here, in which the significant points would be the victories of Peter the Great over Turkey and Sweden, the campaigns of Münnich and Apraxin, the defeat of the King of Prussia at Kunersdorf in 1759, and the occupation of Berlin by Russian troops in the following year; then the brilliant feats of arms in the reign of Catherine, the victories gained by the military genius of Suvorov, the war of 1812, the final defeat of Napoleon, and lastly the part played by Alexander I (thanks to his genuine talent for diplomacy) before, during and after the Congress of Vienna. A place in the front rank of the great powers once attained, Russia kept it throughout the first half of the nineteenth century. The Crimean War marked a certain decline in influence and prestige, but the conquests in central Asia and the drive to the Far East compensated, in the latter half of the century, for the sensible mortifications sustained in the West. The West, however, had greater importance, if not for the State's own interests, for the country's intellectual life and the general orientation of her subsequent history.

The political conceptions of the old Muscovite State were Byzantine; the idea of the new Empire, that of Peter the Great, came from Rome, and therefore from the West. When he founded the *Senate* in 1711, the Tsar must have had something more than Sweden in mind. Ten years later the senators invested him with the titles of *Pater Patriae, Imperator, Maximus*. The difference between the internal structure of the two states corresponds with that which is evident enough in the dominant ideas of their respective foreign policies. Not that there could

be any complete rupture here. However resolutely it might
turn its face to the West, the new Empire was not free to renounce its Byzantine inheritance. There has been no change in
the geographical and racial conditions of its development; the
links that bound it to the Slav peoples and to the Orthodox
Church were still strong. Hence came one of the chief tendencies
of its diplomacy, in the eyes of the West the most important of
all: it was that which from the reign of Catherine II gave
birth to the "Greek project", and was to give rise in the next
century to the ideology, clamorous but politically ineffective,
of "panslavism". The dream was hardly realisable, and in
fact it was not realised: the "Holy Greek-Slav Empire" (as
Tyutchev called it) could not be founded, nor the cross placed
anew on the dome of Santa Sophia. On the other hand, the
realist policy of the imperial government in the Balkans produced excellent results from the European point of view, even
more than from the strictly Russian. Thanks to this, the hold of
Turkey on the Christian peoples of the peninsula was relaxed
and finally removed. It is a mistake to think—as is sometimes
still done in the West—that this policy, or even the panslav
ideology (so different from the Teutonic pangermanism),
aimed at anything in the nature of a conquest of Europe.

Russia had been a great European power from the time of
Peter. As such she found herself on occasion in conflict with
other powers; in the Crimean campaign she had them all on
her back at once. But it was impossible to imagine her ranging
herself against the whole of Europe *on principle*. On the contrary,
if there was any constant element in her policy, it was her
devotion to the idea of a European system, to be maintained,
developed, and defended against every threat. Paul I sent his
troops under Suvorov in an attempt to save what he conceived
to be Europe from the destruction that menaced it (as he
thought) from the French Revolution. Alexander I was the
principal promoter of the Holy Alliance and had long had
dreams of an international order that might ensure to Europe
an enduring peace. Nicholas I meant to have this order respected by all means in his power. He would even have recourse,
once again, to armed intervention: in 1848, to defend Denmark

against the designs of Prussia, he went so far as to declare that if necessary he would occupy Silesia and East Prussia; or again, he put an end to the Hungarian rising without any attempt to exploit it in the interests of Russia. One can have, very obviously, quite a different idea of European order from that conceived by these three emperors; but it is impossible to deny that they took this order seriously, or that Nicholas I in his rôle of policeman was quite disinterested. To this constant preoccupation must be attributed also the initiative of the last Tsar, which on 18 May 1899 led to the summoning of the first Hague conference, the result of which was the founding of the International Court of Justice, a foreshadowing of the idea of the League of Nations.

The sense of Europe that dictated this policy of the imperial government showed itself also, and in a highly paradoxical manner, in its attitude to the territories conquered from the West. Its share in the Partitions of Poland was admittedly a crime as well as a blunder, though Russia, so far from taking the initiative, merely followed the example of her western neighbours and (at any rate after the first partition) annexed only provinces where the population was Russian. More striking than this was the policy of Alexander I, not only towards Poland, which he gained from the third partition and the Napoleonic Wars, but also towards Finland, conquered from Sweden in 1809, and the Baltic countries, attached to Russia in the course of the previous century. To Poland he granted the liberal constitution that, in spite of his promises, Russia awaited in vain. Finland received at his hands the political autonomy that had been taken from her by Sweden. The serfs were liberated in Esthonia in 1816, in Courland in 1817, in Livonia in 1819; the rest of the Empire had to wait till 1861. The régime of Nicholas I, so relentless against liberty in the interior of the country, never wholly reversed the policy of the preceding reign in its dealings with the western marches. That is true even of Poland, whose constitution underwent no radical change till after the second insurrection, in the reign of Alexander II; yet this reign, on the other hand, was in all respects favourable to the liberties of Finland. It was only under

Alexander III that the policy of whole-hearted russianising was adopted; and this, continued in the next reign, was in flagrant contradiction to the Empire's traditions. There was a widespread feeling in Russia that this policy would have to be abandoned. During the war, the Grand-Duke Nicholas was induced to promise Poland her independence, and in 1917 one of the very first acts of the provisional government was to reaffirm the autonomy of Finland. Indeed the lack of understanding, in regard to these problems, shown by the last two Tsars and their immediate associates arose out of a certain faltering in their idea of the Empire, not out of any change in their attitude towards Europe.

THE WEST IN RUSSIA

From the Russian point of view, the history of the last two centuries is the history of the mingling of Russia and the West. At its origin there were two movements: the urge of Russia towards the West, and a drive of the West into Russia. In some respects the second was more powerful than the first. Russia needed the West; while safeguarding, on her side, her territorial gains, what she desired above all was to adopt the technical achievements, and also the arts and learning of the West; this aroused in her a curiosity, more or less intelligent and more or less profitable. The west, on the other hand, rushed to a kind of *levée en masse* and, without taking much thought, flung itself into the project of a total conquest of Russia. This, to tell the truth, called for no armed adventures, no initial design and not even the vaguest strategical plan. It was purely an economic and cultural conquest. Throughout the eighteenth century and a good part of the nineteenth (the movement slowed down later, but it never changed its character), we have a peaceful invasion of Russia by pioneers from the West, all taking good care of their moral and material profit, but all capable of teaching her something, of providing an example of one thing or another, of organising her activities, superintending labour and creating works of some value.

There was a veritable rush of scientists and scholars, of

engineers and technicians of all sorts, architects, painters, musicians, singers and dancers, specialists in the military or culinary arts, teachers and governesses, fops and courtesans and even footmen—the latter, at a pinch, being prepared to teach deportment or, for that matter, letters. The academies of science and the arts, the universities and schools, the large factories and all the departments of the civil service, were in the early days so many western colonies, the function of which was to be the nurseries of the new Russia. By the middle of the eighteenth century, the number and influence of foreigners was so great—especially, but not entirely, in the capital itself—that saturation point was reached and a reaction set in. From 1750 to 1850, the form and direction of this reaction often changed, but not its essential function. Whether it was Lomonossov, warring against the Germans in the Academy; or the satirists of the reign of Catherine II, denouncing the gallomania of the court and the town; or Admiral Shishkov under Alexander I, setting up as a grammarian and endeavouring, somewhat crudely, to purge the Russian language of neologisms borrowed from the West; or again the first slavophils, seeking to preserve the national characteristics of Russia from blind and destructive westernisation—what all were trying to do was to establish an equilibrium, upset or threatened by Peter and his uninspired successors, whose methods had been over-hasty, too crude, or unnecessarily rigid. If they were mistaken, or if they exaggerated in the opposite direction, their work was not in vain. For the danger they sensed was a real one. There was a certain type of "European" Russian that was not very desirable or profitable to the country. Such people lauded the West only to evade their duty to Russia; they boasted their knowledge of foreign countries and foreign languages only to excuse their knowing nothing of their native country and to justify their abusing their own mother-tongue. Even quite recently, Russians who had never seen the Caucasus would visit the Alps every summer; those who knew nothing of the best artistic periods in their own country would be loud in their admiration of Boecklin or Meissonier. This irresponsible escapism, if it had not been checked, might have had disastrous consequences.

By losing what was personal and unique in her possessions as a nation, Russia was also losing her right to a place in the community of Europe.

The danger was averted, but the invasion of Russia by the West still had far-reaching consequences. Peter's appeal to the "Varangians" resulted in the significant fact that for the next two centuries Russia had few eminent men who were of pure Russian descent. The élite of the new Empire was not formed without a considerable influx of foreign blood. Indeed in more than one respect the Empire and its capital could be regarded as hardly more than outposts of the West: outposts where some of the former glories of the West enjoyed a kind of posthumous blossoming. It was thus that Russia preserved the classical ballet at a time when it was rapidly decaying in France and Italy, the countries that gave it birth; it was thus, too, that the great architecture of the West came to flourish in St. Petersburg, for the last time before its death; it was thus that, in the works of Jukovski, Batiuchkov and Pushkin, the best poetical tradition of old Europe bloomed again. But for a completer view of the importance of the West in Russian life, there are two particular influences that must be carefully distinguished: they were the most powerful and at the same time the most violently contradictory—the influence of France and that of Germany.

The French influence, in the eighteenth century the most potent of all in every country of Europe, completely dominated the life of Russia, intellectually and artistically, from the accession of Elizabeth to the death of Alexander I. In many ways it has continued right down to our own day. For nearly two centuries French was the first foreign language learnt by all Russian children of good family. The greatest poet of the country confessed he was more familiar with French than he was with his own tongue; it was the language he preferred to use for his love-letters, for his official correspondence, and even for his private notes when there were abstract ideas to be expressed with clarity. Russian taste in the arts, until the years when it began to degenerate and from the moment it again became purified, allowed itself to be guided entirely by the French.

Russian thought and the Russian language grew more supple and precise by submitting to this particular intellectual discipline—the most precious gift, in every age, that France has always contributed to the civilisation of Europe. But in one important sphere, that of political theory and the organisation of the State, this influence clashed at a very early period with the conflicting influence that came from Germany, and first of all from the Prussia of Frederick the Great. The famous reversal of alliances after the death of Elizabeth was due to the absurd admiration for the King of Prussia conceived by her successor, Peter III. Paul I inherited this admiration, or adopted it, rather, out of resentment against his mother; and once he ascended the throne he imposed the goose-step on his army—and also on his ideas. His son, Nicholas I, was the typical Prussian officer; he administered Russia wholly on the German model, and it was he who made of it what Bakunin called a "knouto-Germanic Empire". In this, Germans (whether Baltic or not) had such influence that General Ermolov, the hero of 1812 and Viceroy of the Caucasus, proclaimed for all to hear that he proposed to ask the Tsar for "promotion to the rank of German". Broadly speaking, if throughout this period the cultured class in Russia was attracted by French political ideas —those of 1789 and 1848—the State itself and governmental circles preferred to be guided by German methods. And it was German socialism that finally triumphed at the expense of French socialism in the revolution conceived and effected by Lenin.

The war of Franco-German influences is a good example of the difficulties Russia faced in assimilating the western heritage, so complex as it was and full of contradictions. Apart from this, too, there was the great difficulty of knowing what to take and what to leave alone, how to distinguish between borrowings that were profitable and necessary and those that were incompatible with Russia's national existence. Tyutchev very nearly hit the nail on the head when he wrote (in French): "A great inconvenience we suffer from is having to call 'Europe' what should properly be called 'Civilisation'—its rightful name." His remark would be entirely accurate if he had said ". . . call 'the West' what should properly be called 'Europe'." The great problem was to learn how to feel European from the fact of being and feeling like a Russian. Through conceiving Europe merely in terms of its western characteristics, or even of the characteristics of a particular nation of the West, superficial minds were content to *appear European* and surrender themselves (for instance) to an absurd Anglomania, whereas those who thought more deeply were ultimately led to despair of their own country. This pessimism never became acute till later, but even Pushkin declared: "It was the devil who had me born, intelligent and talented, in Russia." A deep and wide knowledge of western culture led some of the best and least accommodating to anxious doubts about the value of their own. To the question they now began to ask for the first time—How can one be a Russian?—they could find, it would seem, no satisfactory answer. It is this that is reflected in the attitude of a notable émigré in the time of Nicholas I—primarily a quite negative attitude, and not to be explained by purely political causes—the highly cultivated Pecherin, who went so far as to express in verse (otherwise undistinguished) the hatred he felt for Russia, a hatred inspired by disillusioned love:

> *Solace it is to hate one's native land,*
> *To yearn for her annihilation,*
> *And in her ruins eagerly behold*
> *The dawning of a universal spring!*

The balance was restored—somehow. Thanks to the efforts of a few men of genius, and of an élite that was still homogeneous and energetic, harmony was achieved between the western and the national elements in Russian culture, now an integral part of European culture. But this harmony applied only to culture in the stricter sense, to the peaks (as it were) of the national life; it was incapable of penetrating the totality of that life. One of the origins of the revolution lies there; for the revolution was a disguised revolt, not against the West, but against the values that are common to all the national cultures of Europe and thereby assure its unity.

THE GREAT AGE

The integration of Russian culture in Europe was primarily due to the untiring labour and creative powers of a poet. "Peter threw a challenge to Russia: Russia accepted it by producing Pushkin." To-day we can complete this epigram of Herzen's by saying that ultimately the work of the Tsar was a failure, but that failure is unthinkable in connection with the work of the poet, and the continuation of that work by his spiritual heirs. Pushkin, by his genius, is akin to Raphael and Ariosto, to Racine, Vermeer and Mozart; spiritually, he was no less closely allied to Goethe and Stendhal, and to the other great Europeans who were mostly his elder contemporaries and the last surviving citizens of a Europe in process of vanishing. It was to this Europe that Pushkin turned with all his heart and soul: not to the Europe of the future but to the Europe of the past. He was heir to its richest treasures, its noblest memories and its deepest loves. His mission was to make this European past the spiritual home of the Russia of the future. He read the great western poets in order to acclimatise them to this new country; he absorbed the genius of France and England, of Germany, Spain and Italy, so that no region of Europe should be strange to Russia any longer. The task was brilliantly accomplished; but it had to be continued, in his own lifetime and after his death, in a changed atmosphere that he had scarcely known and would never have desired to know. It was an atmosphere of crisis and conflict, that of the nineteenth century, in which the history of the West was to reach its highest peak—and founder.

This century, for modern Russia, is what the age of the Renaissance was for Italy, what the end of the sixteenth century and the seventeenth were for Spain, France and England, what her classical and romantic periods were for Germany. This does not mean that the nineteenth century in Russia was wholly disconnected with the European nineteenth century; merely that it has a different place in Russian history from that which it occupies in the history of the rest of Europe. It was only in the course of it that Russia came to occupy effectively her particular place in the community of Europe, a place corresponding to the essential tendencies of her past. Entering upon this new phase of its historic destiny, Russian culture for the first time attained its full individuality, and this in the midst of a greater whole though not one that was lacking in form or limits. It was by participating fully in the life of Europe that Russia became fully herself. But this came to pass in the century when Europe itself was gradually ceasing to be that which it had always been in the past. By becoming part of that Europe, now in process of transformation, Russia necessarily shared in all its uncertainties, its discords and confusions. Hence the complexity and contradictions in Russia's *grand siècle*, so strangely different from those of the West, yet wholly untypical of the nineteenth century as it was experienced in France and Germany and England. The close connection of Russia with the glorious past of Europe led to the expansion of Russia's own national culture. But her links with contemporary Europe made that expansion somewhat troubled, lacking in balance and full of sinister apprehensions. The Russian rebirth was the birth of a tragedy; it is this that distinguishes it from the rebirth of the various countries of the West.

Russia produced, in this period, a very great wealth of things vital and elemental: the genius of Tolstoy alone is a sufficient example of it. And this wealth, perhaps actually surpassing that of the West, she was so far from keeping to herself that she scattered it throughout the length and breadth of Europe. Nothing could be more Russian than the thought of Soloviev, the music of Mussorgski, the art of Tolstoy. Dostoevski was as Russian as Shakespeare was English or Pascal French; but, like them, the more deeply he was rooted in his own nation the more he belonged to Europe, and to the whole of Europe. In France and England, the conditions that made possible the emergence of a Pascal or a Shakespeare were realised far sooner than they were in Russia; yet Dostoevski seems the contemporary of Shakespeare quite as much as of Dickens, of Pascal as much as of Baudelaire; and as for Tolstoy, he is an epic poet transplanted, by a strange freak, into the era of the naturalistic novel. Russia was young, as the western nations were no longer young. She was young because the centuries before Peter the Great hardly counted. He made her change her aims, her manners and her language; the time when his father had reigned seemed as remote as the reign of St. Louis in France. To anyone looking back, the seven centuries of ancient Russia shrank to the dimensions of a legendary infancy: an iron age, in the eyes of some; but in the eyes of others, and an increasing number, a golden age. The idealisation to which these latter succumbed may be naïve; but it is not to be attributed to any sense of a decline (as is the case with medievalism in the West), but rather to an access of new strength. It was in the West that creative inspiration was on the wane. Here, in this virgin land, or this land that had now become virgin once again, it arose, blew strong and carried all before it, like a wind springing up on some vast open plain.

Yet the restless young giant, still somewhat raw, was no longer a stranger among the older nations. Russia lived her great age when the cultures of Europe were closer together than ever before; she herself, joining in, helped to make them still more so. What might appear, even to-day, as a strangeness in Russian culture, something impenetrable and irreducible, is merely an illusion due to accidental causes. Other nations of Europe have found it equally difficult to understand one another. Few Frenchmen have a genuine appreciation of Milton, or of the Elizabethan drama; few Englishmen or Germans can really acquire a taste for French classical tragedy. If Europe, on the other hand, has not fully assimilated the great Russian writers of the nineteenth century, the fact must be attributed either to a lack of translations, to the indolence of its readers or their ignorance of the Russian language. In principle all these works, of which the most outstanding are very well known, are almost equally accessible to every educated European, because their authors, by the very essence of their genius, all belong to Europe—the Europe that was or the Europe yet to be.

On the very threshold of the century the work of Pushkin summed up all Europe, modern and medieval. On the other hand, after Pushkin, all that was created in Russia sprang as much from him as from nineteenth century Europe. Russian literature, from Lermontov and Gogol to our own day, has its origin wholly in the spiritual revolution effected by romanticism. It was itself part of it and continued it; it never repudiated its heritage. Russian music, from Glinka onwards, owes more to western music (especially post-Beethoven) than to the musical folk-lore cried up so much by the nationalist ideology of some of its eminent representatives. Russian painting—even that which, in painters like Ivanov, Surikov or Wrubel, remained in some respects faithful to sources that were deeply if secretly religious—never found its way back to the old ikon-painting; it expressed the national spirit only by assimilating the modern western tradition. Russian philosophy takes its starting-point in Schelling and Hegel; science was bound to follow western science; theology itself owes as much to western theological and philosophical traditions as to the theological inheritance of eastern Christendom. All this is not due to mere imitation, but to the discovery of a natural kinship. That is why the opposite influence, that of Russia on the West, is simply Europe's receiving back its own soul, enriched and somehow rejuvenated by what Russia has been able to contribute. In the last fifty years of European literature, there have been no names more thoroughly European than those of Dostoevski and Tolstoy; and the spirit in which writers like Turgenev or Chekhov have been read by Englishmen or Frenchmen is far from being that of mere infatuation for exotic forms of art, like Japanese prints or negro sculpture. If Europe came to understand the great creations of Russian culture and to love them, it was no escapism but a re-discovery of its own true image.

"Europe, like Russia, is our mother—our second mother. We still owe her much and we shall owe her more in the future. We have no desire to show ourselves ungrateful." These are not the words of an ardent "westerniser"; their meaning transcends that of traditional polemics: it was Dostoevski who wrote them, shortly before his death, in his *Writer's Diary*. It was his final hope, his last prophetic vision: Russian messianicism it may be, but drawing its strength from a profound faith in Russia's *European* vocation. For Dostoevski, Russia is a better Europe—a better Christendom, if you will—called upon to save and regenerate the other. It matters little that the hope was vain or the faith unjustified; what does matter is that men who were so inspired did in fact turn their faces not to the East but to the West, for they firmly believed that it was for Europe that this new light must shine, a light essentially both Russian and European. What they failed to realise was that, in so far as it was possible, they themselves had already fulfilled the prophecy. This new European alliance between Russia and the West is nowhere better expressed than in the famous words of Ivan Karamazov, when he declares his intention of weeping over the "dear dead" in the "European cemetery". Actually the cemetery he conjures up is also the cradle of modern Russia, the indispensable soil of its spiritual growth, and the "dear dead" are dear only because they belong to Russia as much as to the West. What Ivan Karamazov did not say—a thing that escaped Dostoevski also—was that the great Russians of his age were not merely the guardians of Europe's past; they were the builders of a destiny that should have been achieved one day in the perfect union of Russia and the West, within the framework of a Europe that is the fatherland of both. The miracle they hoped for was never to take place, but thanks to their efforts Russia became a nation among the other nations of Europe, indissolubly bound to them, at least in respect of her creative work. And as we look back on the past, whatever may happen in the years to come, we can never any more eliminate her voice from the rich symphony of European culture.

III

THE CRACK

THE nineteenth century, as we have seen, was Russia's *grand siècle*; but when we consider the whole trend of the two hundred years that separate the death of Peter I from the murder of Nicholas II, we see at once that in the course of this period the ascent was not constant, that a movement in reverse set in, and that the critical point at which the change took place was somewhere between 1835 and 1845, or—to be more precise still—between 1837 and 1842. Not that the second phase was less productive than the first, any less rich in achievement. There is no doubt at all that the contrary is true. But its colouring, one might say, is somewhat more sombre; the air we breathe seems to be charged with thunder; there is a lurid light of fire on the horizon. The joyous hopes, shared by all at the beginning of the century, now gradually disappeared, to be replaced by something entirely different: apprehensions, in fact, of impending calamity. Doubts were entertained about things that in the days of Catherine II, or Alexander I, had never been questioned: the work of Peter the Great, the very foundations of modern Russia, the future of the nation and the Empire. The building, it is true, still looked very imposing; a vast work was being accomplished, great achievements were taking place in every sphere of activity. It was difficult to grasp, at first, precisely what was wrong. For the evil was insidious, lurking deep below the surface; what was actually seen—as all seemed to be agreed—was splendid.

THE TRIUMPH OF PETERSBURG

From the time it first came into existence, the new capital was the obvious symbol of modern Russia. It was all in vain that the partisans of old Moscow sought to bury it under a mountain of obloquy. "Petersburg will perish", "Petersburg will become a desert"—prophecies such as these were often stealthily whispered; but at first, it would seem, they were not widely believed. The city continued to grow, in population and extent, and to embellish its appearance with surprising rapidity. In the eyes of all the world, the work of the great Tsar was the heart of his vaster work: the new Russian Empire. Herzen was to say later that the only relic possessed by Petersburg was the dwelling-place of its founder. This was not true, for the founder himself had had transported to it the relics of Prince Alexander, canonised by the Russian Church and surnamed Nevski for his victory over the Swedes on the frozen Neva. But the error contained a truth, because the capital's real shrine was not the monastery, where these remains reposed in a great silver reliquary, but a mean little wooden house that the Tsar had had built and had subsequently lived in. In the time of Nicholas I the Prussian general Friedrich von Gagern described the house as having the air of a chapel, where the great man was generally venerated "like a saint". The words sound strange to-day, reminiscent as they are of that other sanctuary, also made of wood, though less modest in intention and less humble in appearance: the mausoleum of Lenin in the Red Square at Moscow.

The old capital was quickly eclipsed by the new. Gifted architects built it churches and palaces that could rival the best classical and baroque works of the West. The Smolny Monastery and the Winter Palace of Rastrelli, Voronikhin's School of Mining, Zakharov's Admiralty, all have their claims to be genuine masterpieces. Moreover architects of a lesser stature, even those from abroad who had never built anything of importance before, now surpassed themselves here, inspired by possibilities that were everywhere offered them in amplitude of space, freedom of choice, abundant material and a general zest for building. Puibusque, author of the *Letters on the Russian War*, who came to Russia under Napoleon and stayed there till his death, sums up the work of the eighteenth century in these words: "I know nothing comparable with St. Petersburg for magnificence; here is a uniformity of grandeur and elegance that has no existence anywhere in Europe." But in spite of the splendour of Elizabeth and the pride of Catherine, in spite of the imagination of Paul I (at times somewhat feverish) and the good taste of his Empress, it was only in the following reign that Petropolis really attained the peak of its splendour.

In 1812 Moscow burned: what appeared to arise from its ashes was St. Petersburg, more sumptuous and splendid than ever before. This phantom city—"the most fantastic city," as Dostoevski was to call it, "with the most fantastic history in the world"—the capital founded on a marsh, whose hasty construction in an unhealthy climate had cost the lives of thousands of workmen, was now one of the fairest in Europe, rich in palaces and monuments of all kinds, and housing some of the finest picture-galleries in existence. Situated on a river, beside which the Tiber, the Seine and the Thames are nothing but the humblest of trickles, the capital was thus described by Joseph de Maistre in his *Soirées de Saint-Pétersbourg*: "The Neva flows, with brimming banks, through the heart of a magnificent city: its clear waters lap the lawns of the islets in its course, and throughout the whole extent of the city it is contained by a pair of granite embankments, running straight as far as the eye can see, a magnificent feature repeated in the three great canals that traverse the capital. There is no model or imitation to be found anywhere else."

So it appeared in 1809. Presently the last of Europe's great architects, Carlo Rossi (1777-1849), was to make Petersburg that extraordinary northern metropolis where, under a pale sky and lost amid vast horizons, there were to triumph for the last time the five orders of Vitruvius, the columns and porticos of the Ægean, bordering squares and wide streets that were all too huge for them, and set off by walls of straw-yellow, bilberry or pale green plaster. It is true that when you walked along the riverside quays on one of those nights in early summer that never grow dark, when the very granite seemed to melt into the colourless sky and the columns were but pale shadows in the chiaroscuro that challenged the eye and overwhelmed the spirit, then the city seemed unreal, and through tenuous palace walls you could fancy you saw the boundless plain going on for ever, the infinite expanse of humble peasant Russia. But the dream had gained substance; it had taken flesh, and the city was there, after a hundred years, more than ever before.

The young Emperor had conquered Napoleon and entered Paris in triumph. It was to him the Bourbons now owed their throne; it was he, with Metternich, who at the Congress of Vienna was to order the destinies of a Europe finally pacified. Never again had Russia such a sense of glory and power; at such a moment, patriotic exuberance was understandable. Never again did the Empire founded by Peter the Great seem so firmly established, or that other creation of his genius, Russian society, so prosperous as now, and so active. The country-folk, during the war, had shown an almost religious devotion to the person of the Emperor and a stubborn love for their native land. There was talk of the abolition of serfdom, already envisaged by Catherine; there was even talk of a constitution. Officers, returning from France after the war, had brought back liberal, even revolutionary ideas. Nor did they allow themselves to be discouraged by the change that ensued in the political opinions of the Tsar. After his death they attempted a revolution. The insurrection of 14 December 1825, severely put down by the Emperor Nicholas, had been entirely the work of the nobility. The people themselves had taken no part in it; they never understood what it was about. So they remained silent; and their silence is perhaps something even more tragic than the reverse sustained by the nobility. It showed the desperate unreality of the salvoes of cannon on the Senate Square, of the deportations to Siberia and the executions of the ringleaders—an unreality like that of the city where it all happened, or of the empire of which the city was the figure and symbol—in comparison with the vastness of the Russian land.

Here, once again, a passage from Joseph de Maistre is to the point: "The equestrian statue of Peter I is erected on the banks of the Neva at one of the extremities of the vast Isaac Square. It almost seems that, as he scowls over the river, he gives life to all that shipping his genius created. In this proud theatre, everything owes its existence to a thought in that powerful head which conjured forth from the swamp all these sumptuous monuments. On these desolate banks, from which nature appears to have banished all life, Peter set his capital and created his own subjects. Over their descendants, cowering about the base of his proud effigy, his dread arm is still extended; looking at it, you find it hard to decide whether there is protection or menace in that hand of bronze."

It was about this statue of Falconet's that Pushkin wrote his profoundest masterpiece, that prophetic summary of Russia's destiny, *The Bronze Horseman*. It is the noblest and most impassioned hymn that has ever been sung on the magnificence of Petersburg and the glory of Peter; but there is also a hint for the first time, thanks to the justness of vision that genius alone attains, of the great conflict and essential drama that underlies the whole history of Russia. The Tsar's adversary in the poem is not one that could ever be his equal; he has neither the bravery nor the intelligence of the December insurgents; he is merely a poor wretch, craven and featureless, wholly inarticulate, the starving lover of a girl who has perished in one of those autumn floods, so common in Petersburg, and so dreaded. His misery is his only ground for daring to apostrophise the Tsar sitting motionless on his horse, to shake his fist at him, proclaim his hatred and his terror, and then flee, stricken with madness into the night, through the echoing deserted streets of the city, and pursued in his delirium by the clang of hoofs as the implacable builder gallops in pursuit.

But was this triumph of the Tsar's, the triumph of Petersburg and the Empire, to be permanent?

THE REVENGE OF MOSCOW

The answer to the question is plain enough to-day, but it was much less clear in Pushkin's time. Yet even while he lived there were forces at work that were highly disquieting to those whose hopes and ways of life were all bound up with the work of the Bronze Horseman. It was at first as though a veil had shrouded the ancient landmarks; there then made its appearance something entirely different: a new set of men, a whole layer of the population, that had never before had a part in forming political or social ideas, and now threatened to upset, or alter very radically, the inner equilibrium of the nation.

It was roughly ten years after the December rising that there appeared the first symptoms of a disease that no one yet had clearly diagnosed though its existence was quite unmistakable. It was a time when the political life of the nation was completely stagnant and the autocratic régime of Nicholas I seemed likely to remain unchanged indefinitely. In 1836 Peter Chaadayev, a former officer of the Imperial Guard and a friend of Pushkin (though his elder by ten years), published in a Moscow review the first of a series of *Philosophical Letters*. In this he questioned the inner logic of Russia's national development, sadly contrasting her obscure and fragmentary past with the infinitely richer and prouder inheritance of the West. His views on her future were also gloomy in the extreme, and the Tsar was so incensed that he had him declared insane; the review was banned and the rest of the *Letters* never appeared. Yet this subversive talker (as one would expect, he wrote only in French—it was a translation that was published) was far from rejecting the general tendencies of modern Russia. He wanted to see it, not less, but more European—or rather more definitely western—than it had been growing during the past hundred years. He was the first theorist of any calibre in the "westernising" camp. The westernisers asked nothing better than to follow the course marked out by Peter the Great: to complete what he had begun, but quite otherwise than had been understood by Peter's successors on the throne. In other respects Chaadayev's ideas were very different from his disciples', in so far as these were destined to be politically radical. His mission was simply to unfold a dialectic, the thesis of which is no more important than the antithesis it was soon to provoke.

This antithesis was also the reply of Moscow to the prestige gained by the capital in recent reigns—a very high prestige, but also (as some might contend) artificial. After the very definite and severe magnificence of the palaces framing the Neva, what strikes the traveller, in the public and private buildings of the same period in Moscow, is that their columns and entablatures seem somehow softer and less geometrical; it is as though they had all been drawn without compass and square; in their homely and unstudied grace they have the air of being half asleep. They suggest already the wooden porticos of the old manor-houses, surrounded with their great gardens and buried away deep in the Russian countryside. The reason is, that Moscow has always been closer to that countryside, literally and figuratively, than Petersburg has been. She has remained the capital of the Russian land, the fatherland of the peasants and also of the landowners, themselves closer to their serfs, and with a better understanding of their life and manners, than the officials of Petersburg and the courtiers of Tsarskoie-selo. The nobility of Moscow was at once more patriarchal and more liberally minded than that of St. Petersburg. Its children were given the best European education that there was to be had in Russia at that time. Hence there grew up, among the young men who frequented the salons where Chaadayev was still supreme, a school of thought directly opposed to his own teaching. Its inspiration, like his, was drawn from western thought, but the arms thus acquired were to be used against the West itself.

The first slavophils (for this was the misleading name by which they were known), all disciples of the great German philosophers from Fichte to Hegel, were the first supporters in Russia of a more liberal, cultured and enlightened nationalism. Khomiakov, like the brothers Kireevski and their followers, proposed to interpret Russia's destiny on lines very different from those which Petersburg and the Empire had apparently conceived and laid down once and for all by their decrees. According to them, the true foundations of Russia's cultural and social life had to be sought in the customs and institutions of her peasant people and in the historical remains of ancient Russia. The people and history were their idols, just as with the German romantics—the whole of "slavophilia", as a system of ideas, has an origin that is frankly and exclusively German. They disapproved of the work of Peter the Great, seeing it merely in its destructive aspect. And it was this that attracted the fire of their opponents and started the controversy that has gone on ever since. However, important though the division was, what at first was even more important still was that neither of the two sides adopted for its own the official ideology of the Empire; hence neither was regarded with any favour by the government. Moreover they had various points in common; the necessity of abolishing serfdom, of making a wider appeal to other classes than the nobility, and of encouraging the Russian people to spontaneous activity by the bestowal of free institutions—these, according to the one side, to be popular in character; according to the other, western. And what united them still more was that both formed a conception of Russia and her needs that was poles apart from that which was to linger for years—like a still potent ghost—in the chancelleries of the capital which both were now refusing to recognise as genuinely representative of the country. A poem of Khomiakov had described it, as long ago as 1832, as "a desert of granite, proud of its dead beauty". Gogol himself played the game of the slavophils when he declared: "Russia needs Moscow; Petersburg needs Russia." On the other hand Herzen, in the opposite camp, though he held Moscow to be useless and Petersburg indispensable, declared that the latter, though necessary, could never inspire affection.

Slavophils, no less than westernisers, always looked at their country with its future in mind; but there was now a rift between that future and the present: it was not an immediate prolongation of the present, as it had been for the contemporaries of Catherine or Alexander. Herzen was mistaken in thinking it was only he and his associates who had the prophetic spirit, whilst their opponents were simply living on their memories. Actually the cult of memory, preached by the slavophils, was only the projection into the past of their most fervent hopes for the future. For both parties, Russia was a country incomplete, where "all must be created", as Pushkin himself had proclaimed. He also made it clear, in a note he recorded in 1822, that it was only a revolutionary who could really love Russia, just as only a writer could love the Russian language; for what each would love would be the respective potentialities of language and country. But, while invoking the future, Pushkin had never despaired of the present; indeed, in his riper years, he was inclined to condemn the somewhat impatient ideas of his youth. It was only after his death that hope for the future was the only confidence left. So it was, thirty years later, with another great poet, Tyutchev, who belonged to Pushkin's generation but lived twice as long. He was a friend of the slavophils, a monarchist and a strong patriot; yet he could slip into a letter that he wrote to his wife (still, of course, in French) a little phrase of highly revealing irony: "This dirt of our beloved country, so full of promise!"

THE COMING OF THE CLERKS

There is nothing more striking, in the whole history of Russia, than the kind of underground subsidence that took place just when she seemed to be at the peak of her flowering. In his *Literary Souvenirs*, Turgenev remarks that it was impossible to admire both *The Bronze Horseman* and *The Cloak*. But Pushkin's poem, written in 1833, was published for the first time in the posthumous edition of his works that came out in 1837, the year of his death; Gogol's tale appeared in the same year as his *Dead Souls*, 1842. It is therefore between these two dates that we must set the decisive moment of crisis. As for the impossibility of admiring simultaneously the story and the poem, this was due less to their striking differences as works of art than to the incompatibility of their respective outlooks upon the world. Pushkin saw things as though he were himself raised aloft on the granite pedestal of Falconet's equestrian statue; Gogol looked at them from down below, with the eyes of the wretched outcast whose soul he reincarnated in the hero of his story. Turgenev went on to observe, as another sign of the times, the rapid decline of what he quaintly calls the "pseudo-solemn school", by which he understood a group of poets, painters and writers that might have been the semi-official spokesmen, in their various arts, of imperial Russia at the height of her glory. By now they had played their part; no one listened to them any more. The author of the *Horseman* himself, for all his reputation, found enemies after his death. As for the school of poetry that derived from him, it was to degenerate very soon into a bloodless and academic "art for art's sake". Other writers appeared, among them Russia's greatest, but they had nothing to do with the objects Pushkin celebrated, the Winter Palace or the Admiralty Needle. Their soul is different; they seem to belong to another nation altogether than that which was continuing to wage its wars (less successfully than before), and to conclude its treaties (rarely advantageous); the nation that continued to exalt in solemn language, which now sounded hollow, the unbreakable bonds that united Church and people and throne all in one; that still sped over the highways of all that vast Empire those "forty thousand couriers"—the phrase associated with a comic character in Gogol.

For the most part these new writers still belonged to the nobility, but there were already others of humbler extraction in their ranks. Not having received the careful education that the State reserved for the nobility, these brought to literature somewhat ruder manners, a less chastened style, more summary judgments, and a fashion of controversy without respect for their opponents. As time went on the difference became less marked, or disappeared altogether; higher education was to become accessible to all; the shock that had been caused by the advent of these outsiders, became softened to a mere memory. Their coming, nevertheless, was something of the first importance in the history of Russia. It marked the rise of a whole new stratum of society and the parallel decline of another; also—what is most important of all—it marked the end of that homogeneous élite which ever since Peter the Great had presided over the destinies of the country. Russia's governing class, from this time onwards, was wholly distinct from its cultural élite. There was an inevitable lowering of the moral and intellectual standards of the former: as for the latter, it either turned away from politics altogether, or else directed its political activities against the government, which ultimately meant—since the government was identified with the State—against the State. Thenceforward there was a complete rupture, not simply between the "real" and the "legal" country, but between Russians and Russia.

"We made an experiment," wrote a shrewd observer,

General Fadeyev, thirty years later, "that was contrary to everything in our modern history, by dissolving our élite into the mass before giving it time to act freely and mature; now we are seeing the first consequences, but by no means the last, in a general moral disintegration." This is no recrimination of a dispossessed member of the privileged class, but the objective recording of a very disquieting state of affairs; for the lack of a homogeneous élite, and the division that ensued between those who governed the State and those whose duty it was to think and create, were bound to conflict with the normal and healthy development of the nation. Russia never quite succeeded in recovering her inward balance, upset by this serious crisis in her growth. She remained a rich and powerful country, developing in some respects with surprising rapidity; but the deep wound in her refused to heal; there were times when it bled and became increasingly visible. There was a general feeling of uneasiness, a dull apprehension of unknown disaster. The descendants of the men who had built modern Russia were themselves incapable of building any more; they had neither the necessary tools nor the necessary faith.

Towards the middle of the century the new Russian élite, now sharply distinct from the governing class, very quickly took shape and acquired its special designation, the *intelligentsia*. This borrowed word, hastily incorporated into the language, indicated that it was composed of intellectuals, or more simply of the educated. They belonged for the most part to the various liberal professions and by birth might just as well be nobles as peasants (very rarely the latter) or, what was more common, the sons of merchants, artisans, priests or minor officials. But what they all had in common was neither profession nor social status but—a thing without parallel in the formation of an élite—a steady and (as it seemed) automatic opposition, not to the Emperor, the court or the government, or any particular tendency of that government, but to all that might be described as "official" Russia, to the whole political and social framework of the country. By virtue of a tacit convention observed by this new "clerical estate", no one was thought eligible to belong to it who was either a priest, an officer, or a civil servant, however brilliant and well-informed such a person might be; equally barred, as a rule, was anyone whose opinions seemed in the least reactionary or conservative or even merely moderate, susceptible (if they were known there) of being approved in high places. There might be a considerable difference between a university professor, elegantly critical and liberal, and a bomb-throwing terrorist who was a candidate for the gallows; but to be admitted to the bosom of the new élite, the condition that was at once necessary and sufficient was at least a minimum of subversive spirit. This, then, was the perfectly clear attitude of the élite towards the State; the problem of its relations with the people is rather more complicated.

One of the most convincing signs of the real failure of Peter's work is the fact that in Russia the idea of the people was much more potent than that of the nation. Doubtless all culture involves some injustice: especially a high, vertical culture, when all around there is only limitless plain. Hence a feeling of remorse. The bronze horseman was only metal after all, he might well be thrown away; his victim, on the other hand, was humble and living flesh; and men fell down and worshipped him. In the second half of the last century the very people who should have staffed the nation, directing it and making their achievements its own, turned towards the people with a gesture of humility, brotherly compassion—and abdication. The new clerks were joined by many young men and women of the governing class: a whole "repentant nobility", as it was called. The movement itself (it should be called *demophil* rather than *populist*) is one of the finest that the history of any country has known. It is evidence of a perfect disinterestedness, a rare keenness of moral sense, a deep and sincere desire to repair old wrongs, even going so far, if necessary, as to give life itself to relieve the sufferings of those whose toil and pains are the basis of all society. Its primary source was most certainly Christian; and more precisely evangelical; it inspired every Russian writer after the conquest of the West. Yet the movement was highly destructive. A master-builder, who gives up the work on which his ancestors before him have laboured for generations, who proceeds to beg his masons' forgiveness for having placed himself at their head, and hands them his plans and drawings so that they can finish the work without him, gives proof of considerable generosity and high-mindedness; but he must own that in this way the building will never be finished, and that he is therefore guilty of treason, not only to his predecessors but still more to the work itself—the work that after all was his own responsibility and thanks to him will now fall to ruin.

Soloviev was quite right, when he wrote at the end of the century: "The greatest act of human justice in all our history would never have been accomplished if people like Radishchev and Turgenev, Samarin and Miliutin, had had the fancy to become peasants, as Tolstoy did: if they had taken to the plough and begun working the land instead of fulfilling their literary and political duty." But for others than Tolstoyans it was not so much a matter of taking the plough as abandoning the rod, of laying down the compass and the square—and fighting those who retained these implements. As for the great "act of justice", this was the abolition of serfdom and the later liberal reforms of Alexander II; but the period of understanding, even partial understanding, between the clerks and the administration was of short duration; and an understanding—namely a true community of effort—with the real people, that is with the peasantry, soon proved to be wholly impossible. Two months after the manifesto that liberated the serfs (that of 19 February 1861) the very Youri Samarin that Soloviev mentions, a prominent slavophil, an ardent promoter of reform and one of the most intelligent men of his age, wrote to a friend in Petersburg about the peasants he knew so well and for whom he had worked so hard. His letter throws light on the thing most fundamental in the great Russian problem.

He confesses that what had struck him most, in the course of his talks and negotiations with the peasants about the manifesto, was their utter lack of confidence in anything that emerged from the State and in those who represented it in any capacity at all, "in all that half of Russia that is not the people". The peasant was willing enough to obey, but he declined to understand. "Manifesto, uniform, official and ukase, the provincial governor, the priest with his cross, the will of the sovereign—for him all these are lies and trickery." He would put up with it all, as he put up with heat and cold, but to none of it would he give his assent; he would do nothing at all with spontaneous conviction. "It is true," adds Samarin, "that he cherishes an image of the Tsar, dwelling in Petersburg, a being infinitely remote from himself. But this is not the Tsar who is the real ruler of the country; he is a mythical being possessed of semi-divine majesty, one that any impostor could successfully impersonate to-morrow." So the country was still slipping out of the hands of the townsman who tried to seize it, and the horizontal culture, weaving its unending carpet, still escaped that other culture, the one that builds stores and railway-stations—and also cathedrals.

The people were distrustful, as always, of the State; but they were equally distrustful of the new clerks and repentant nobles, who opened their arms to them and sought, as they might, to win their confidence. The efforts of the State and the intellectuals, whether concerted or independent, failed to produce results that were at all deep or lasting. Tolstoy retired to Yasnïa Poliana, where he devoted much of his time to the school he had founded for the children of those who had been his family's serfs; he wore a peasant's blouse and boots, and would feed no better than the peasants fed. Young intellectuals would traverse the countryside, trying to interest village youths in ideas they had borrowed from the latest and most "advanced" of socialist pamphlets—hastily translated from the French or German. At last, on their side, the government and even the imperial court sought points of contact with the peasantry; under the last Tsar especially, much time was thus occupied at Tsarskoie-selo. Rasputin's boots and blouse were not, after all, so very different from Tolstoy's; and the former, at any rate, was a genuine moujik. But peasant Russia knew very little of Tolstoy, nothing at all of the imperial court. Youthful propagandists were sometimes found, by the roadside or on the edge of some forest, with their throats cut. After the good years of Alexander II, and still more after his death, the struggle between the State and the revolutionary *intelligentsia* went on as barrenly as ever, and more and more implacably, on the surface of the vast land that lay all the while impassive, slumbering in a heavy and dismal silence.

WORN-OUT SYMBOLS

At the beginning of a long, unfinished and lucidly tragic poem, Alexander Blok, the greatest poet of the new century, described its predecessor as the "iron century". Yet it began more happily than any other for Russia, and brought her more glory than all the rest put together. Even when a third of it had passed and all suddenly turned dark, it remained the "great" century, as we have already seen; only its aspect, as reflected in its works, was no longer as it had been at the beginning, serene, full of confidence and contentment. It was now either sombre and contorted, rent by incessant inner conflict, or else it suffered from a kind of nostalgia, exhausting and incurable, a despairing hope that was projected out of reality into illusion and dreaming.

Gogol relates how Pushkin, just before his death, after having had read to him the opening chapters of *Dead Souls*, exclaimed: "God, what a sad country our Russia is!" It was the feeling that obsessed everyone: Gogol himself, and Chaadayev in his worldly solitude; Pecherin, the brilliant professor, who quitted his chair for ever and his native country; Herzen the émigré, and the poet Nekrassov; the young Turgenev, the young Dostoevski and the young Tolstoy. It was like the rending of a veil, that suddenly revealed the weakness of all that had before seemed powerful and glorious. It was then that the emblems of Empire, the firm symbols of its duration, could be seen to be wearing away and crumbling to dust.

"You ask me how I like Petersburg," wrote a young Balt to his brother. "Cold magnificence, vast soulless buildings, a city of stone; it lacks that circulation of the blood which is life to cities like Paris or London. Built in its northern desert, it may soon be like the ruins in that other desert, like Baalbeck or Palmyra. Petersburg is an artificial city that rose rapidly out of nothing, and when the Russian Empire is no more it will collapse just as quickly. It is a city that has no existence in its own right, by virtue of its site or history; it exists only because it happens to be the residence of the Russian Emperors." This letter of Victor Hehn's was written in 1835, two years after Pushkin wrote *The Bronze Horseman*. Even before this, as we have seen, Khomiakov had talked of its "dead beauty". On a visit to the capital, he had called it a "city where all is stone: not only the houses but the trees and the inhabitants." "If only for a single day," exclaimed Custine some years later (in 1839), "this capital without roots either in history or in the soil is ever forgotten by its sovereign, if its master's policy is directed elsewhere, the granite hidden under the water will crumble away, the flooded lowlands will return to their natural state and the inhabitants of solitude will regain possession of their home."

Thus ancient prophecies came to be born once more. "No one believes any longer," says Custine again, "that this marvellous capital will endure." While the youthful Hehn was writing to his brother, while Pushkin was at work on the manuscript of his poem, Pecherin, the future émigré, was working on a tragedy that turned on the punishment of an unworthy people whose capital perished by flood. About the same time, so we are told, Lermontov was in the habit of sketching, in pencil or water-colour, the waves of a stormy sea, from which there emerged the peak of that commemorative column which Alexander I had erected before the Winter Palace. And again, after Lermontov's death, it was Herzen, in 1843, who wrote: "The life of Petersburg is wholly in the present: it has nothing to remember but Peter I; her past was manufactured in the course of a century, and having no past it has no future either; any autumn it can expect the squall that will finally wreck it." And it was not enough merely to foretell it; the shipwreck was something to be desired and actually sought for. In the course of the years that followed, the prestige of the capital declined with astonishing rapidity. It had ceased to be "marvellous"; it had become ugly and commonplace. The slavophils overwhelmed it with sarcasm and insults, like Ivan Aksokov, who wrote to Dostoevski about 1860: "The first condition for recovering our feeling of nationality is to detest Petersburg with all our strength and with all our soul; we must spit upon it." This was no doubt an attempt at outbidding, but in a novel of Pissemski's, that appeared in 1858, a far from excitable character is made to call it a city "without a breath of fresh air, without history, nationally featureless"; and Turgenev himself in his *Phantoms*, published some years later, described with melancholy disenchantment, verging upon disgust, its wide streets, grey and deserted, its miserable shops, its fortress-like walls of granite, the crumbling stucco of its palaces, its smell of dust, sauerkraut and stables. Anyone might think it was always thus it had appeared to the world, drab and gloomy, doomed to early destruction.

Yet Petersburg itself had not greatly changed; only nothing had been built, after the death of Rossi, that added anything to its beauty. What had grown unrecognisable was the way it was regarded by the best minds, even by those, now rare, that retained any affection for it. Dostoevski had never ceased to love it, and time after time he describes its atmosphere unforgettably; yet even he viewed it differently as he grew older. In 1847, in a forgotten article that recently came to light, he still contested the opinion of Custine, who blamed the capital for a lack of architectural unity. His reply was that Petersburg was the heart of Russia; that it was still in process of construction, and therefore covered with plaster and dust; that the idea of it, conceived by Peter the Great, was not yet realised but would be in the future; that it was growing stronger every day, not only on the actual banks of the Neva but in the country as a whole, which physically and spiritually depended solely on Petersburg. Fifteen years later his opinion had changed; at the end of a further fifteen it had become remarkably like Custine's. In a private note, made in 1876, he expresses astonishment that the Austrian Emperor should have found Petersburg so beautiful, denies that it possesses any character of its own, and declares that if the city were discovered, a thousand years hence, like a new Pompeii, it would be impossible to guess what sort of people had lived in it or what their ideas could have been; and since it had a little of everything, but nothing peculiarly its own, the question would remain for ever unanswerable.

The various modes of regarding Petersburg, and the way they contrast at different periods, are an important indication of the destiny of modern Russia. When, for Dostoevski, it takes on more and more the aspect of an illusion, a mirage that will one day fade into the mist and leave nothing behind (as we read in *A Raw Youth*) but the old Finnish marshland and in the midst of it the Bronze Horseman on his panting steed, we feel sure that all this stands for the Empire as well, and that he had much less faith in its strength and durability than he had had, as we have seen, some thirty years before. In another note he jotted down, in 1873, he hints at how the illusion may end, in a general rising and a change of régime; and again he bethinks him of the Horseman, as if stressing the fact that he is not separating the destiny of Petersburg from that of Russia, as Peter wished it to be, as Peter founded it. "I have often asked myself," he wrote, "how, apart from a political cataclysm, anyone could decide to abandon palaces like these. And as to that, what would become of Petersburg if it were abandoned? The Germans would remain, and a crowd of stuccoless houses with nothing to keep them up, their windows broken, and in the midst of it all—the monument of Peter."

What Dostoevski saw, others saw also, only with less penetration. And other symbols besides Petersburg were perishing at the same time, and at a similar rate, all gliding down the same slope. The Tsars themselves, as time went on, became less and less like their mighty ancestor; their court lacked the brilliance and splendour of Catherine the Great's, Alexander's, or even that of Nicholas I. Their life was more bourgeois; in quest of comfort they lost a taste for the magnificent; with signal ineptitude they sought to become "popular", while losing contact more and more with the real *people* of Russia. In the end it seemed natural enough to find the imperial family affecting a great love of simplicity and an infatuation for rustic pleasures. On the eve of the revolution, the dwellers in the sumptuous palaces of Pavlovsk and Tsarskoie-selo were distempering their bronzes and mahogany in bright colours, replacing furniture by Riesener with bamboo screens and maple wardrobes, covering up their chandeliers and removing their damask, tricking out their windows with neat cretonne curtains and decorating their walls with picture-postcards, stuck fan-wise on priceless brocades.

THE REVOLUTION ON THE WAY

To understand the ideas behind the revolutionary movement in Russia, and still more its psychological background, it is not enough to study the history of socialism and the revolutionary spirit in the West; such a study might actually be misleading unless it included also the Russian writers of the nineteenth century. It is true that the ideas which fostered the Russian revolution were all without exception of western origin. But the thing to grasp, if one is to penetrate deeper than vague international phraseology, is the way these ideas were understood, assimilated and experienced in Russia; and nothing gives so fair and complete an image of this as the literature of the country at the period when these ideas were in full process of development. It is true that the great Russian writers were no more on the side of the revolution than on that of the State, but they all considered it as an authentic and formidable force, in the sphere of action and also in the sphere of thought. They too had all experienced these revolutionary ideas, each in his own way, and Dostoevski more than all: his *Possessed*, in fact, is a prophetic vision of the Russian revolution. As to the truth of the picture in terms of the contemporary realistic novel, we have enough facts to prove it; Dostoevski can hardly be said to have "exaggerated" at all when we compare his heroes with such historical characters as Nechaiev or Tkatchev: the first served as a model for the coldly destructive fanatic, Peter Verkhovenski; the second is notorious for having proposed quite calmly to make a final end of despotism and secure the triumph of the revolution by exterminating, as incapable of assimilating the new ideas, every Russian of either sex over the age of twenty-five.

What *were* these new ideas? In their purely political aspect they could be identified with the programmes—the most radical programmes—of the western revolutionaries; but the foundation on which they rested, the deep springs from which they originated, were not the same. When such ideas entered Russia they took on, almost at once, the aspect of nihilism: an attitude of mind that has nothing to do with sceptical or relativist principles, or even with those positivist beliefs that have been at the back of all the western revolutions. It might rather be defined as a burning faith in Negation, or better, perhaps, as a passionate affirmation of the worthlessness of everything that had been generally held of value in the spheres of religion, art or morality. Anything that had no purely animal value in relation to such necessities as food or sex was regarded by the nihilist as meaningless and non-existent. But the proclaiming of this non-existence, the mere destruction of values, was itself, in his own eyes, the supreme value of all, a value for which he was even prepared to sacrifice his life. Thereby he created a kind of religion in reverse, for which he was perfectly willing to offer himself as a martyr. As a religion in reverse, it authorised assassination and recognised nothing specially sacred in the human personality. But it was none the less a religion: it provided its followers with the certitude and courage that are necessary for action—and heroic action. And the Russian terrorists it formed were often ascetical and pureminded, saints of the black halo and the blood-stained dagger.

It was a direct consequence, this nihilism, of an ideological complex widely prevalent in the Christendom that ever since the eighteenth century had been really de-Christianised. This complex might be described as rationalist obscurantism. Now what is original in the Russian revolutionary movement is just its pushing this ideology to its ultimate limit and drawing from it conclusions that others had abstained from drawing. Rationalist obscurantism may sometimes be nothing more than a mild expression of human mediocrity, extolling a reason it is very far from possessing. His own well-being is the chief concern of your suburban secularist; not his irreligion, which is something to air, rather than a principle of conduct. But only some of the excesses of the Combist madness in France can suggest any idea of the militant positivism that flourished in the Russia of 1860 and 1870. For a Russian, these years evoke a whole atmosphere, and one that is peculiarly their own; an atmosphere of ingenuous materialism and intransigent utilitarianism; of compulsory acceptance of "advanced" ideas, which meant the rejection of everything incapable of being demonstrated, in a couple of minutes, to minds of extremely limited intelligence; the maintaining that Shakespeare is complete rubbish, that the metaphors of poetry are just shameless lies. At the same time, the idolatry of science, the inevitable corrolary of rationalist obscurantism, produced in the Russia of this period a stubborn hostility to anything like free scientific research. What in the West was only a hypothesis, here became a dogma; any hypothesis opposed to it was regarded as heresy. To a follower of simplified Darwinism like Pissarev, anyone of the Lamarck school was a traitor and an outlaw. It was Pissarev, too, perhaps the greatest single influence on the younger generation, who vented spiteful gibes at Pasteur's experiments, which refuted the spontaneous germination of microbes.

To minds like these, philsophy, art and humanism were all bound to be suspect. Chernychevski, quoting one of Pascal's less happy thoughts, declared that a real apple, by the very fact that it was edible, was in every respect preferable to a painted apple. Pushkin, Lermontov, Turgenev—all were subjects for debunking. Pushkin, in *Eugene Onegin*, had talked of "frosty dust"; in winter, they objected, after snow there could be no dust. For Tkatchev, *War and Peace* "would be a dangerous book if it were not for its mediocrity"; another liberally minded critic saw in it nothing but "an oafish corporal, relating his military exploits to the clowns of his village". Saltykov, a novelist himself, describes *Anna Karenina* with an expression we can only translate politely as "a gynæcological novel", while a still more radical publicist bids Saltykov himself put aside his futile literary exercises and devote himself exclusively to popularising natural science. As one might expect, any condemnation of such modes of thinking was instantly denounced as a reactionary outrage against the sacrosanct "young generation": namely against those young people who, as Tyutchev justly remarked, were "all more or less infatuated with the rights of reason, for which they were all the more concerned the less they made use of it."

This great mental clean-sweep, this carefully prepared blank, was indispensable if nihilism was to assume its final form, which was that of terrorism. Such a necessity, however, required a pledging of the whole being, that would serve as a kind of tragic consecration. And it was not mere negation or hatred that spurred the terrorist to action; there was something positive as well, that never derived from theoretical nihilism. Like the "repentant noble", the village schoolmaster or the doctor who attended his patients without fee, like all the *intelligentsia* that sacrificed itself to what it believed to be the interest of the people, the nihilist also, as Soloviev so rightly observes, acted on the strange line of argument: "Man is descended from the monkey, so let us love one another." Scratch the terrorist and you discover the philanthropist; continue to scratch and you will end by discovering the Christian gone astray. These were the men of good will who pursued so remorselessly, and ended by killing, that other man of good will, the Emperor Alexander II. Well might he cry, as he did one day: "But why on earth are these wretched men all against me? Why do they track me like a wild beast?" The liberal reforms of the early part of his reign were the greatest constructive work of the Russian State since Peter the Great. The very day he was killed he had just approved the project of Loris Melikov that would have led to the establishment of a representative régime. But between the government and the revolutionaries, between the *intelligentsia* and the State, no understanding was any longer possible. When the Tsar emerged unhurt, after Rysakov's bomb had wrecked the imperial coach, and the two men confronted one another face to face, what could have been their thoughts in that brief instant before the second bomb (thrown by Grinevetski whom it killed) tore off the legs of the "liberator Tsar"? A few hours later he died.

That first of March, 1881, was a decisive date in Russia's history. Thenceforward the struggle was equally cruel on both sides, and equally senseless. The government sent young students to Siberia for a single attendance at some innocent demonstration and thereby, of course, made them revolutionaries for life. Terrorists, sometimes mere children, would murder not only administrators hated by the people, but also honest officials who were personally blameless, and (quite promiscuously and automatically) officers of the gendarmerie or policemen—all to manifest their hatred of the established order. There was a notable decline, towards the end of the century, in the country's intellectual vitality. This was due to what may be described as the double censorship. The official censorship ran amok and committed ludicrous blunders; but there was another and even more formidable censorship, exercised by a tacit understanding in the opposite camp. It was conducted by all the "progressive" papers and reviews (others, by common consent, were barred by all decent people), which either attacked ferociously, or ignored with stubborn silence, the works of any writer who refused compulsory tribute to revolutionary trivialities. Turgenev, Goncharov, Dostoevski, Tolstoy—none of these escaped the vigilance of this second censorship; other writers of considerable talent—Leskov, Leontiev, Pissemski—were all during their lifetime persecuted remorselessly. Even to this day, thanks to its posthumous influence and to a certain inertia of opinion, they are not occupying the place that is rightfully theirs in the history of Russian thought and literature.

So the struggle went on, and the whole Russian élite, that which still carried on the government and that which belonged to the *intelligentsia*, became exhausted in the course of it. The last two decades of the century were marked by a general fatigue, a stagnant routine, and that strange loss of hope and any faith in life which is reflected so well in the works of Chekhov. There was expectation in the air: the anxious expectation of irrevocable disaster; and resentment, too, at its delayed arrival. But fundamentally it was there already, though no one could see it. It was not due to the government's failure in its struggle with the intellectuals, not to the failure of the intellectuals in their war against the government; it was due to the failure of both, the failure of that part of Russia capable of thinking, acting and struggling, in coping with the great mass of the Russian people. The new Russia was about to perish of the same weakness as the old: the inability to hold and penetrate and influence all that people, scattered over the boundless unmeasurable plain. There is an increasing air of aimlessness, as though none of those responsible for their country's destiny had the least idea where he was going. A poet like Tyutchev, endowed with a keen political sense, had been aware of it since the end of the reign of Nicholas I. And his uneasiness was not limited to what he considered the alarming features of the Crimean War. The truth of the words he wrote to his wife, on 13 June 1854, became much more apparent thirty years later: "What is so bewildering is the conviction—and it is becoming more and more general—that in all the perils that confront us the direction of affairs is given over to a way of thinking that no longer has any understanding of itself. It is like being in a carriage, descending an increasingly precipitous slope, and suddenly realising there is no coachman on the box."

IV

INTERRUPTED RENEWAL

EVERYTHING seemed to indicate, about the close of the last century, that Russia would remain permanently in a state of stagnation and eventually succumb to that strange kind of stupor, like a soft and gently suffocating blanket, which seems to envelop the world of Chekhov. But the ways of history are always more devious than anyone would expect; even in a mortal illness there may be a time when life takes a last revenge, unexpected alike by patient and physician. What happened did not obviate the final disaster, or even, in all probability, delay it; this went on brewing, in the apparent calm, and when it came at last, twenty years later, it was brought about, at any rate in part, by events that were quite extraneous. But the expectation was largely veiled from the eyes of contemporaries by a revival they had reason to think might well be enduring, possibly even final.

The twenty years that preceded the revolution were culturally such a period of growth and flowering that compared with the golden age of Russia, that of Pushkin's lifetime, it may justly claim to be her silver age. It was not only a religious, artistic and intellectual renewal, but a renewal of the State itself, of the structure, social and economic, of the Russian Empire. But we can see to-day, looking back after the event, that considerable as they were these changes were not enough, that they affected no more than the shape of the building—the building which, for good or ill, had been in process of construction on Russian soil since Peter the Great—but not the soil itself, which remained shifting and unstable, less capable than ever of supporting what was imposed on it. So it was that after it had been raised a little higher, consolidated and repainted, completely redecorated inside and out, after witnessing twenty years of the most brilliant achievements in literature, science and the arts, the ground again subsided and the building collapsed.

THE ECLIPSE OF NIHILISM

The October Revolution ultimately derived from nihilism, even though the latter, at the end of the last century, was in process of rapid decay. It was only for a brief period that it dominated the intellectual life of Russia, and when it perished it took with it all that had been associated with it: rationalist obscurantism, the absolute primacy over other human interests of particular social and political problems, and the subjecting of literature, the arts and the spiritual life generally, to the interests of revolutionary propaganda. All this disappeared, but not completely or instantly; traces of it could still be found in the succeeding years; but what had occupied, if not the summits, at any rate the uplands of Russian culture, descended now into the valleys. The intellectual level of Chernyshevski, of Pissarev or Dobroliubov, was sensibly lower than that of men like Herzen or Bakunin, their predecessors in the ways of revolutionary thinking, and they are in no sense great figures in Russian literature or thought; but after their death even this level was never again attained in their camp. The ideas were still there, but no longer the ability; talent was elsewhere, travelling by ways that were freer and more varied, venturing to concern itself with other things than politics. A new period was beginning; and it was only when the revolution was finally achieved that there was a return to such clichés as "problem" pictures and literature of the politico-moralising sort—things that fifty years ago were relegated to the attic, where one might reasonably have expected them to remain for good.

For a student of the revolutionary history of Russia it is interesting to notice that the decline of nihilism coincides with the *intelligentsia's* being initiated into Marxism; but from the point of view of the history of Russia, particularly of its thought and culture, the most important fact is that from 1900, at latest, neither nihilism nor Marxism, nor even the revolutionary movement itself, was any longer fashionable with thinkers and artists. Among that rich and brilliant generation of the élite which came to maturity about the close of the century, there were three young men who had been violently attracted by Marxism: Peter Struve, Nicholas Berdyaev and Serge Bulgakov. But Marxist teaching was only a phase they went through, and one they quickly grew out of. The first, an eminent economist, became one of the most cultured and most independent thinkers in the Russian political world; the second abandoned Marx to construct the philosophy, based on Christian metaphysics, to which he owes his present reputation; the third was converted at the beginning of the century, was ordained priest in 1918, and became in due course the most eminent modern theologian of the Orthodox Church. These three names are perhaps the best symbol of the profound transformation of the Russian élite that took place on the eve of the new century. Marxism, it is true, still had its faithful adherents, but from the point of view of the history of thought, and in so far as this is to be distinguished from history pure and simple, these latter may be said to be negligible quantities. The revolution was the work of men who believed themselves to be Marxists but were in fact the direct heirs of the revolutionary nihilism of 1860; the renewal, on the other hand, was brought about by men who had repudiated Marxism and nihilism alike, and were consumed with the desire to draw their sustenance from the authentic sources of the spiritual life.

In spite of all the dryness and oppressiveness of the last century, these sources were never stopped, they had merely flowed underground, to emerge here and there with all the greater vigour. The thought and art of men like Tolstoy and Dostoevski, as well as of other great nineteenth century Russians, was deeply rooted in the Christian faith of the people. It was this that isolated them from the intellectuals of the positivist school; yet it somehow failed to draw them closer to one another, or even to the people whose deepest life they unknowingly shared. In order to be propagated, their thought needed interpreters who could bring it into the common patrimony of Russian culture. Of these the first and most diligent was Mereshkovski. Similarly the influence of the great religious thinker Soloviev never really began till after his death in 1900. Writers like Khomiakov, Leontiev or Fedorov, were never truly appreciated till the beginning of the century. In the 'sixties, the Leftist censorship would have had no difficulty in stifling any work as original as Rozanov's, shattering as it did so many "progressive" dogmas; it could no longer do so in 1910 or thereabouts. The year 1903, that saw the founding of the Society of Religious Philosophy and also of the review *Novy Put'* (The New Way), is an important date in the history of Russian thought: it marks the end of the old bigotry in reverse, of the prejudices, anti-religious and anti-philosophical, so rampant among the intellectuals of the previous generation. Symbolism, dominant in Russian poetry between 1900 and 1911 or '12, meant something very different from what it did in France, and in the essentials of its message it has more in common with German romanticism. The symbolist movement had national roots in the work of Dostoevski, Tyutchev and Soloviev. Its greatest poet, Alexander Blok (who admittedly, in his latest period, came to abandon the æsthetic doctrines of that school), had begun as a poet of mysticism and remained faithful always to certain religious themes that are associated with what is deepest in Russian tradition. Generally speaking, the whole spiritual background of those years was steeped in religious aspirations and a tendency to mysticism, affording, if only in this, a striking contrast to the previous age.

The Orthodox Church itself awoke and took its part in the renewal. Its cultural level had been high for some time and the instruction given in its more advanced schools—the four theological academies—was comparable to that of the theological faculties of the West. Outstanding personalities appeared among its clergy, which itself began to play a more active part in the general life of the nation. The Church studied its own past, acquired a better understanding of its potentialities; it took a belated account of its great theologians of the previous century, Khomiakov, Bukharev and Soloviev; this enabled it to achieve an even fuller intellectual revival in the work of men like Bulgakov and Florenski, and so gain far greater influence on the general intellectual life of Russia. And it became much less self-confined; it explored the idea of a reunion of the churches and became aware of its own mission within Christendom as a whole. There is nothing more striking about the

Russian tragedy than the fact that the revolution, which was later to endeavour (vainly, it is true) to exterminate the Church, began by furthering one of its most imperious needs: it allowed it to throw off the yoke of the synodical régime that for two hundred years had stifled the freedom of religious thought, and to convoke, for the first time since Peter the Great, a Pan-Russian Council for the election of a patriarch. Such an event, looked forward to so long, would have been out of the question in the moral atmosphere of the last century. This revival of the Church, and of religious life, was symptomatic of a fresh impulse in all the creative faculties of the country and also of a profound change in the inward structure of its cultured class.

THE TREASON OF THE CLERKS

The partial or complete abandoning of what had recently been considered in Russia as the immortal principles of 1860 could not fail to disorganise the ranks of the *intelligentsia*, previously so firm and so confident of their mission. Those among its adherents who were attracted by the new ideas were regarded by the rest as deserters to reaction; at the same time, the stalwart intransigents could not fail to seem old-fashioned to the younger generation and to those of their contemporaries who were determined to be up-to-date. The revival was the work of a new cultural élite, as entirely distinct from the old intellectuals as from the noble and bureaucratic "high society", borrow though it might some of its elements from each. Both these groups proved extremely resentful and often took a strong dislike to the innovators, all the more because the latter were drawn from every social class and were extremely varied in their opinions and talents. A man like Chekhov was unambiguously of the *intelligentsia*, just as Tolstoy had belonged to the old aristocracy; but it was difficult to class under either of these headings a painter like Wrubel, a musician like Scriabin, poets like Annenski or Sologub or Blok, or most of the scholars, artists and writers prominent in the Russia of the twentieth century.

By virtue of what seemed to the survivors of 1860 and the

fanatical revolutionaries a veritable treason of the clerks, the cultural élite in Russia was tending to become just what it was everywhere else: a social stratum distinguished by a certain degree of education and by its function in relation to the rest of society, not by its political opinions or its adherence to any ideology held in common. This tendency was one of the most important features of Russian society and Russian culture in the years immediately preceding the revolution. Previously, as we have seen, a learned priest, an officer of outstanding literary attainments, a scientist who was also politically "retrograde", were none of them regarded as belonging to the *intelligentsia*. Now the very meaning of the word began to alter; what it was coming to signify was all who possessed some intellectual distinction, who had attained a certain standard of education; it implied nothing else. The very type of the old-time radical intellectual was becoming by this something of a figure of fun. He was still encountered on the stage, and sometimes in real life, with his pince-nez glasses and goatee-beard, ascetically thin, slovenly in dress and voluble of speech. The intellectual of 1910 bore no resemblance, even outwardly, to the 1860 brand. Even if he was a political revolutionary, he was not so in the same way. He no longer read the same books or referred to the same authorities. Above all, his culture was infinitely richer and more varied. Chernyshevski's novel, *What's to be done?* was no longer to him a literary masterpiece; in judging literature and the arts he no longer used the criteria of Pissarev or Dobroliubov, or even of Bielinski, a sacrosanct figure to several succeeding generations of intellectuals. There were more things he was interested in, and this made him at once more tolerant and more adaptable, more capable of compromising with reality and much more disposed to create than destroy. The new cultural élite was Russia's great hope at the beginning of the century; but there were still forces at work to hinder its maturing, and the old ways of thinking, which it tended to destroy, simply descended now to a lower stratum of society.

The new generation, that arrived on the scene on the eve of 1914 (or 1917), could count in its ranks a far higher proportion, than it could ten or fifteen years before, of youngsters who had received only the most summary education, whose intellectual luggage consisted of no more than a little cheap science and political ideas which they were satisfied were "advanced", culled from handbooks they had read quite uncritically. A number of these had received higher education, but without having followed a regular course at a university. Only a certain proportion of students read seriously; the rest organised "meetings", took part in demonstrations, tried to make themselves as awkward as possible to the government and to those of their professors whose revolutionary sentiments seemed not above suspicion. Most universities were closed during the political troubles of 1905. Afterwards there was more work done to make up for it, but there were always those students of the "eternal" type, culturally underdeveloped, who worked only under protest and talked all the louder. These, with numerous other second-rate intellectuals, formed a kind of sub-élite that was to provide the backbone of the revolution when it came.

It was this sub-élite that inherited nihilism and *fin-de-siècle* Marxism. With the single exception of Gorki, no writer of any standing, who began to publish after 1890, owed anything to the ideas that belonged to this heritage; and even Gorki himself, at any rate *qua* artist, appeared to owe less to it in the period of his maturity. When, in the name of these ideas, he protested in 1915 against the staging of Dostoevski's *Possessed* at the Art Theatre, there were many who shrugged their shoulders and regarded it as no more than an isolated survival of the "censorship of the Left"; it was not realised then that it might also be a foretaste of what would happen to Russian culture after the revolution took place. But the survival was not so isolated as it then appeared to those who were working to revive that culture. There were others still to be found in the clichés of journalists and parliamentary orators; also in the methods of secondary education, in which the whole of Russia's literary history was represented as the struggle of "advanced" ideas against those that were not sufficiently advanced.

All that might change; it was already changing. But was it possible to rely on this completely? Could one ignore the mounting wave of "demi-intellectuals", as they were so well described, now being thrown up by the primary schools? These were capable of quite another "treason of the clerks"—if it is possible to be treasonable to a culture one neither belongs to nor respects. Things were made worse by the frequent incompetence and venality of the administration, by the ineptitude of the State in domestic policy and public education, and by the profound indifference of the people itself. It was not those who made the revival that were to unmake it; the danger was to come from others, compared with which they were only a handful: from the countless multitudes of the sub-élite, full of hatred and envy for the true élite. Yet all the same the renewal that took place survived to the revolution, and not all its traces were wholly obliterated by the thirty years of the régime that followed.

THE SILVER AGE

Nihilism had been vanquished, or at any rate dislodged from its dominant position in the time of Pissarev and Tkatchev, not so much, as we have seen, by the direct impact of religious tradition or effort as by the joint action of all the creative energies belonging to the realms of intellect, imagination and faith. The desire to know, whether by the intelligence or the senses, could not be contented indefinitely with the meagre nourishment afforded by rationalist obscurantism. Disinterested investigation, uncontaminated by ideologies, could not be denied for ever to the natural and human sciences. The appearance of thinkers like Soloviev or Fedorov showed that the banalities of vulgarised science, based on positivist principles, had not entirely supplanted all profound and independent philosophical thought. But the most violent reaction against the immediate past was a revolt of feeling, taste and imagination, elements which in the domain of literature and art had previously been regarded as superfluous. It was specially in relation to poetry that the new era had soon to be regarded as a silver age. Its beginning was clearly marked by a revival of artistic forms and new æsthetic ideas.

To the survivors of the old generation, these young en-

thusiasts, writers and artists, were scarcely more than "æsthetes"
—therefore morally suspect, if only for their indifference to
politics. On these grounds they were barred by the revolutionary *intelligentsia*. But if æstheticism is to art what hypocrisy
is to morals, obviously the first depends on the existence of the
second; therefore the arrival of the "æsthetes" was an unchallengeable proof that all artistic life was becoming richer and
more intense. An infatuation for Oscar Wilde and Aubrey
Beardsley, for the Munich *Jugendstil* or the *fin-de-siècle* decadence of Paris, were not in themselves very much to rejoice at;
but no artistic movements are altogether exempt from feeble
excrescences, and all of them involve some new snobbery or
other that they not only encourage but live on. The rich Moscow business-man, converted to the "new Art", was ridiculous
enough as a human type, but at least two of such made admirable collections of French paintings, from Manet to Picasso,
and others contributed very practically to the rediscovery of the
old ikon-painting. They might be irritating enough, the new
ideas and the new affectations, but nothing could be more
legitimate than the reaction they set on foot against the mentality of the old *intelligentsia*. The latter held it positively
indecent even to dress with any care or cultivate any taste in
matters of food or drink, to read poetry or look at pictures, to
have a liking for beautiful books or to show the least interest in
art or letters as such. But the age was theirs no longer. The good
old days of the problem picture and "civic" poetry were now
dead and buried, and it only remained for the muse of Nadson
to shed disconsolate tears over their grave.

The opening of the new era was marked by two foundations:
the Petersburg review, *Mir Iskusstva* (The World of Art), started
by Serge Diaghilev and the painters Somov and Benois in
1897, and a few years later the Moscow Art Theatre, the work
of Stanislavski and Nemirovitch-Dantchenko. During the
twenty years from 1897 to 1917, Russian literature produced
no genius comparable to Tolstoy or Dostoevski or Pushkin or
Gogol, but in all branches of letters the number of talented
writers had never been so great, their public so large or the
general level of its culture so high. For proof of this it is only

necessary to compare the standard of any review or daily newspaper, or even the outward appearance of a book published in this period, with the best of the kind that the previous era could show. At the Leipzig book exhibition, in July 1914, the Russian section was one of the most brilliant, and the very high standard of the graphic arts, due to the contributors to *The World of Art*, was maintained to some extent even after the revolutionary débacle. The painters of this group excelled no less in theatrical décor, the revival of which, throughout the whole world, owes much to the example of Alexander Benois and Leo Bakst, to Golovin, Roerich and the whole team of scene-painters who became known to Paris, and indeed to the whole world, after Diaghilev's first season at the Châtelet in 1909. The flowering of the art of scene-painting, like that of the graphic arts, depended in its turn on the general revival of the arts of design (including, but not primarily, easel-painting) starting from the generation of artists like Wrubel (1856–1910) and Serov (1865–1911). As for the triumph of the Russian ballet, this was fundamentally bound up with the new impulse given to music by the pupils of Rimski-Korsakov and Taneyev, and above all by Scriabin and Stravinski, and with the brilliant rejuvenation of all the arts of the theatre, drama and opera as well as ballet, the tradition of which last had been continuously preserved, though it flourished now with an intensity and exuberance that was entirely new.

Literature, and the whole literary environment, underwent an equally complete renewal. Poetry, barely tolerated in the recent past, now dominated literary life, became the principal interest of men of letters, and imposed its own laws on fiction and the drama. The first wave of "decadent" or symbolist poets, Balmont, Briussov, Zenayde Hippius, Sologub and (greater than all, but somewhat apart) Annenski, was succeeded by another, which in the work of men like Blok, Biely or Wenceslas Ivanov, gave symbolism a deeper mystical significance; then a third, that of Gumilev, Anna Akhmatova, Hodassevitch, and Ossip Mandelstamm, which was by now in reaction against the technique or even the spirit of symbolism but still shared the rich inspiration of the new poetry. Even the leading prose-writers owed much to it, with the exception of Gorki and Bunin, whose maturest work dates from later than 1914. The novels of Biely, Sologub's *Sly Demon*, the prose of Remizov, Kuzmin or Zaytsev, are the products of a period deeply penetrated by a stream of poetry. Even criticism felt the effects of it, and it is to the efforts of poets and writers, rather than to those of scholars, that we owe the final canonisation of Pushkin, the re-established reputation of Boratynski and Tyutchev, poets hitherto unappreciated, as well as an interpretation of the work of Gogol, Tolstoy and above all Dostoevski, that revealed for the first time their significance and true import. There was a change even in the manner of reading the classics, whether Russian or foreign, and of appreciating the masterpieces of the past. The sense of her own tradition, so long wanting to Russia, now belatedly came to birth and promised to create more stable foundations for the work of the writers and artists of the future. All that Russia could later export in the way of artistic values, all the (infinitely reduced) stock of them she may still possess, is wholly the work of this very short period. And it was an anything but peaceful period: it was disturbed by an unsuccessful war, an abortive revolution and a series of dull shocks that foretold a new landslide and afforded a presentiment of imminent disaster.

The life of at any rate the cultured classes was rich and full during these twenty years. It was also a little feverish, perhaps. Even during the war, on the very outbreak of the revolution, the reading of a new poem by Alexander Blok or Anna Akhmatova was for many an important personal event, a joy or an anguish, an intimate communion with reality. When Scriabin was at the piano, his music evoked an emotion that was very much more than mere æsthetic pleasure. To hear Shaliapin or Sobinov, to see a Meyerhold production or one at the Art Theatre, to be transported once more by that strange voice of the great Komissarjevskaïa, young students of both sexes would queue at the box-offices in their hundreds all night. New writers and artists seemed to be born every day; universities and picture-galleries, every institution devoted to the arts or sciences or letters, were being transformed or modernised under one's very eyes; the country's past was being studied with more love than ever, and with more objectivity. Ikons, the most beautiful painting that Russia had ever produced, were being discovered once more after being forgotten for centuries. Privately, too, there were fine collections being made of pictures and drawings, books, engravings and all works of art; exhibitions, both of ancient and modern art, could always be sure of attracting crowds. Ancient churches throughout the country, ancient towns and dwelling-houses, were now for the first time being gazed on with wonder not only by artists but by ordinary travellers.

The two capitals were living a life of almost equal intensity, and it was now Moscow's ambition to excel its old rival in modernity and Europeanism. Petersburg, in spite of this, recovered her former primacy. In some respects, it is true, its new brilliance was only the reflection of its old-time splendour, and its artistic activities were somewhat retrospective, embracing a number of elements that were borrowed or artificial. But life on the banks of the Neva had its share in the general renewal and none can deny that it was brilliant. The city of Peter the Great and Pushkin was finally rehabilitated: people dwelt lovingly on its past; they studied it, imitated its classical architecture, became more than ever aware of its beauty, of the unique poetry it evoked; it had become, as by magic, the capital of painters and poets. More than ever the work of Peter seemed achieved. The bronze horseman rode triumphant on his granite base and the old prophecies were all forgotten that foretold the end of St. Petersburg and the Empire.

THE LAST CONQUESTS

The impulse did not falter. It was not exhausted by any internal cause; it was broken from without, by forces that belonged to a different scheme of development. It could never be said of the Russian silver age that it either broke up or changed its direction: it simply foundered in the social cataclysm, whence there emerged, not a new culture, but—the U.S.S.R. Moreover its destruction was not immediate, nor is it entirely certain even now that it is final. The development that tended to a closer union with the West, to an integration with it even completer than in the previous century, continued under the Soviet, in a somewhat feeble and sporadic fashion, until somewhere about 1930; and among the Russian émigrés it continues to this day. As far as theory is concerned, there has been a revolt of the "Eurasians" among the émigrés; but actually, since the revolution, what Russians have created of any value looks to the West; it has its roots in a Russia that is an integral part of Europe. This is Russia's only way; certainly it is the only one that can be of any benefit to her in the things of the spirit. And it was in this direction that the silver age was the age of her last conquests.

Contact with the West, somewhat relaxed in the time of Alexander III, in the reign of the last Emperor was intensified and extended. Never before had cultured Russia such a sense of being naturally European, of being a nation with a natural place among the nations of Europe. It was precisely for this reason that Russia became conscious of her national traditions, of her proper spiritual activities and her particular function in regard to the European community. And she had never shown before so lively an interest in the whole *corpus* of western thought, western literature and western art; never had she explored these so fully, never had there been more translations of western novelists, historians and philosophers. In no country, during these years, was there probably such a consumption of contemporary literature and art produced abroad, especially in France, Germany and England, but also in Scandinavia, in Italy and Spain. Writers like Ibsen and Strindberg, when they were hardly known in France, were passionately admired in Russia; on the other hand, French painting and literature were more warmly welcomed than ever and exercised a far deeper influence in Russia than in the countries of the two great writers of the North.

And this interest and enthusiasm was by no means restricted to contemporaries. Once again, as in the age of Pushkin, it was the whole past of the West that literary and artistic Russia desired to annex. An early book of Merejkovski's, studies of the great figures in European literature, was finely entitled *Eternal Companions*; it is typical of the mood in which the Russian élite, no longer bridled by its masters of 1860, read *Faust* or the *Divine Comedy*, or saw its best actors play *Hamlet* or the *Malade Imaginaire*. A brilliant team of young scholars at Petersburg University, direct or indirect disciples of Alexander Vesselovski, embarked on a profound study of the language and literature of the Latin and Germanic peoples. The history of these peoples, medieval and modern, was being brilliantly taught in more than one university. The soil of Italy, sacred already to Boratynski, Alexander Ivanov and Gogol, became so now for innumerable poets, artists and ordinary travellers, who went there every year, in increasing crowds, with a filial piety that begot poems (like the famous cycle of Alexander Blok), novels (like Boris Zaytsev's *Far-off Country*), not to mention travel-books and essays (like Paul Muratov's excellent *Images of Italy*). Pilgrimages were made, not only to Florence and Rome, but to Paris, to the German university cities, to Greece and the whole Mediterranean world, the cradle of Greco-Roman civilisation. For this age, so fruitful in other respects, brought about also a renaissance in classical studies. Its humanist-poets, Annenski, Wenceslas Ivanov and Zielinski, published new translations of the Greek tragic poets and dreamed of a Slav humanism similar to that of the Italian Renaissance, or of Winckelmann, Goethe and Hölderlin.

The Sabashnikov publications, among them that magnificent series of translations, the *Monuments of World Literature*, set so potent an example that imitations appeared even after the revolution: e.g., the *Universal Literature* series, patronised by Gorki and published by the State between 1922 and 1925, and the numerous *Academia* publications that followed later. Reviews like *The World of Art*, *Balance*, and *The Golden Fleece*, were concerned with foreign literature and art quite as much as with Russian. Discussions on East and West, on Russia and Europe, tended more and more to lose their acerbity. Differences were recognised but no longer regarded as irreconcilable. The contrasts were admitted, but stress was laid on natural affinities, on the features that were either harmonious or complementary. Moreover, close acquaintance with the West made for a better understanding of Russia's own past. A study of the medieval West threw an entirely new light on medieval Russia. A love for Italy made it easier to understand Vladimir or Novgorod or Moscow. The "discovery" of French painting made that of the ikons possible. Nothing understood or created during this period would have been conceivable without the existence of this new kind of knowledge, these new enthusiasms and this general broadening of the spiritual horizon.

The new state of affairs was partially recognised by the West, which showed itself at last more forthcoming where Russia was concerned, and paid more attention to the various manifestations of her intellectual activity. There was a poetic justice in this tardy recognition, seeing that in the past it had been Russia who was so eager for western culture. The time had come for Tolstoy, Turgenev and Chekhov to play an active part in the literary life of Europe; for Russian music, Russian dancing and dramatic technique, to renew and even regenerate the musical and theatrical life of the West. The penetration of western culture by these elements, new but by no means entirely foreign, is to-day an accomplished fact and one that it is hard to underestimate. The various events of the last thirty years, however diverting (in the primary sense of the word), so far from arresting or even retarding it have actually tended to accelerate its tempo. Russia is known as Russia no more, and its fallen capital bears very logically the name of him to whom it owes its fall; but in the world of the spirit Pushkin is still Pushkin, Tolstoy is still Tolstoy. Thus Russia's blending with the West goes on, in so far as life itself is not stifled and genuine creation still remains possible.

This is true of the West: it is no less true of Russia. In this respect there is no difference between the U.S.S.R. and the émigrés. In Russia as elsewhere, all the best writers and the only genuine artists, so far from shunning the West, are drawing closer to it than ever and accepting it still more fully. In the U.S.S.R., the only literary generation that was able to express itself at all freely, at any rate at first, was that which immediately succeeded the revolution, the generation of "Serapion's

Brothers", of Babel and Olesha; it was a generation that was frankly "westernising". To this, too, belong the few novelists of talent that have appeared among the émigrés, and they show the same tendencies. The most noteworthy among them, Nabokov-Sirin, is undoubtedly the most western of all who have written in Russian, even in his sensibility and the working of his mind. For the younger generations the pitch has been hopelessly queered in Russia, and elsewhere the game is now hardly played; but there is no reason to think things have changed fundamentally. True literature may be killed by the mass-production of pseudo-literature, and it is this that is slowly happening; but killing is not altering. The same might be said of music and the plastic arts, of philosophy, history and social and religious thought. In all these spheres the renewal, crushed in Russia, continues among the émigrés—feebly, of course, and very obscurely, but recognisably the same. The river is now only a trickle, but it follows the same course; it is only the supply of water that is steadily decreasing. When it dries up altogether, the traces will have to be sought in the sand, for that will be the only way to form any idea, even the sketchiest idea, of the Russia that might have been, were it not for the Russia that is.

SIGNS AND PORTENTS

What might well be called the paradox of pre-Soviet Russia is seen nowhere more strikingly than in the situation in which she found herself during the reign of the last Tsar. For that brilliant era of renewal—it is now time to make this clear—was also a period of very acute crisis. It seemed to be a crisis of growth, but one could be sure of nothing. Was it possible to say precisely just what was going on in those open spaces away from the capitals? The best minds were divided, there were two conflicting feelings: their country seemed on the way to the fairest imaginable future; it was about to succumb to the worst of all disasters. Russia was growing rich as they watched her; she was being modernised and completely transformed; her material and spiritual life was more intense than it had ever been. At the same time, in every nook and corner there were symptoms to be observed of a deep-rooted distemper; the danger could be seen approaching, but none knew how to meet it.

The general situation was all the more obscure in that it was impossible to know from what angle to view it. Government and opposition both lagged behind events. The country was being transformed while the imperial court seemed unaware that anything was happening. After the rough sketch of a revolution in 1905, the political régime had been changed; but it seemed the Tsar and his chosen ministers wanted to ignore it as long as they could. They regarded as null and void what they held to have been extorted. They referred to the people. So did the opposition, and in a fashion no less arbitrary and gratuitous; for the ideas of both sides were equally vague, and equally different from what the people themselves wanted or were capable of conceiving. The political struggle, inside or outside parliament, constitutional or otherwise, went on as it were in a vacuum. Hence there were grave misgivings as to whether any normal development was possible. The resulting pessimism and anxiety were always counter-balanced by the optimistic hope that the rapid changes taking place could not be limited merely to the political sphere, but would result in a total metamorphosis of Russian life. From being an agricultural country with a patriarchal society, industrially and commercially still under-developed, Russia was now becoming wholly different: modern, industrialised, with social and economic conditions similar to those that had existed in the West for about a century. Hamlets were being transformed into great industrial agglomerations; small market-towns, like Ekaterinoslav or Rostov on the Don, were becoming economic centres of the first importance. The urban population, which in 1897 had been no more than 13 per cent of the whole people, fifteen years later could be reckoned at 20 per cent. The ministry of Witte saw the beginning of the Trans-Siberian railway, as well as a whole network of other railways besides, the mileage of which doubled between 1894 and 1905. The total volume of production, five hundred million roubles in 1890, in 1912 was nearly six milliards. So it was not a mere flight of the imagination when, in one of the poems he wrote about this time, Alexander Blok professed to see rising over his country "the star of a new America."

America or no, to what remained of the old *intelligentsia* as well as to the majority of Russia's cultural élite, these rapid material changes suggested that the political and social structure of their country might be approaching that of the great western democracies. From the end of the previous century the revolutionary parties had had to recast their various programmes, since it was now obviously impossible for Russia to escape capitalism; and this, they believed, was bound to lead ultimately to a political régime of bourgeois democracy. They therefore supported the political demands of the liberal and middle-class parties, though seeing a liberal revolution only as a necessary prelude to a socialist revolution. These tactics built up a powerful coalition against the government; and the very breadth of its basis, even for the mildest liberals, was a permanent source of confidence in the future. On the other hand the accumulation of capital in private hands, and the rise of a small but wealthy and cultivated middle class, favoured all kinds of artistic and intellectual activities. The influence of the press increased greatly, a wide variety of new periodicals began to appear; the new middle class was prolific of patrons, collectors and publishers, who powerfully furthered the cultural revival which inevitably, in its turn, inspired confidence in the strength and vitality of that class.

The unfortunate Russo-Japanese War, followed by the revolution of 1905 (which alarmed the moderates as much by its own excesses as by the Tsar's incapacity to understand his own country), had caused this first wave of optimism to subside; but it rose again, two or three years later, higher than ever. The freightage figures doubled between 1904 and 1913, as did those for the output of the foundries, mines and sugar-refineries. Progress in education kept pace with industry. Between 1911 and 1914, the number of children in the primary schools jumped from six to eight millions, that of pupils in the secondary schools doubled in the same period. The general speeding-up of the tempo of life was no less apparent in local government and the vastly increased activities not only of the municipalities but of the rural *Zemstvos* as well. This huge Russian countryside was beginning to alter, to live an intenser and more varied life: a fact that could be attested by the number of peasants belonging to rural co-operative and profit-sharing societies, the membership of which increased in ten years from seven hundred thousand to ten million. And this, incidentally, was the result of a very important reform. Stolypin, Witte's successor as President of the Council, had promulgated a law, in 1906, by which every head of a peasant family was entitled to annex his share of the commons and convert it to his own private property. This was the first step to establishing a new legal status for the peasantry and abolishing the old régime of agrarian collectivism. By turning the peasant into a smallholder, Stolypin hoped to find him a powerful ally against any attempt at social revolution. The reform could not be realised completely; but between 1906 and 1916 three million peasants, 20 per cent of the total, took advantage of the new law to renounce their membership of the rural communities and acquire their individual parcels of land. The rural population was in a very fair way to acquiring a standing, juridical and psychological, that was comparable to that of other classes in the Empire—a thing that might have had incalculable consequences in the future. But, as events soon showed, the beginning had been too late.

The scene darkened once again a few years later, and this time for good. Politically, there was the feeling once more of having reached a dead end. Witte had been finally removed from power. Stolypin was assassinated in September 1911 by a revolutionary who sought to clear himself from the charge of being a police agent. The government paralysed the work of parliament; the opposition in parliament tried to thwart every action undertaken by the government. The universities were hampered at every turn by Kasso, the Minister of Education, while the students, for their part, neglected their studies and had thought for nothing but political agitation. Rasputin, by exploiting the malady of the Tsarevitch, increased his influence daily over the Emperor and Empress. It almost seemed as if the growth of material riches and resources went hand in hand with a kind of moral infirmity. The process of making Russia democratic and bourgeois was not always attended with very happy results. The rise of the "demi-intellectuals", primary school products who were susceptible to the crudest forms of propaganda, was still disturbing the representatives of true culture. Indeed, from the beginning of the century, the impression one gets of Russian life, as reflected in Russian literature at the height of its flowering, is the prevalence everywhere of very sombre hues. Country life was never more cruelly exposed than in Chekhov's *Peasants*, in some of Gorki's descriptions, and above all in Bunin's *Village*. Similarly in Sologub's *Sly Demon* the mingling of the old flat provincialism with the new *petit bourgeois* spirit is presented with a vigorous hatred that is all its own. For Andrei Biely, at the time he wrote *Petersburg*, the Russian Empire with its capital and its bureaucrats, and the terrorists hunting its bureaucrats, is once again the same phantom that Dostoevski prophesied might any moment dissolve into the mist. But it is Blok's *Private Diaries*, for all his vision of a new America, that give the best idea of the deep uneasiness that was gnawing at the loftiest and more sensitive minds. And they were the years when all Europe saw its anxieties and apprehensions steadily increasing.

"Cursed for ever," wrote a Russian poet,[1] "be the year fourteen!" It is highly probable that with no European catastrophe Russia would have found a way out of her difficulties without revolution and destruction. As it was, Russia's destiny was no longer separable from Europe's, and all Europe has reason to curse the same year. In several countries there were those who foresaw the peril and all its implications. After the second Balkan war the atmosphere in Russia became still more tense. Germany's attitude was increasingly aggressive. The policies of Austria and Turkey were giving more and more anxiety both to the Russian government and to Russian public opinion. Then the day came that brought news of the murder of the Archduke Francis-Ferdinand. From end to end

[1] Hodassevitch.

of the vast country the July of that year was one of parching heat. Forest fires broke out; the fumes of the smoke, sweet and stale, brought simultaneous drowsiness and insomnia, and they even penetrated to the heart of the great cities. Work and rest were equally impossible; amidst an agony of anxiety there was a temptation to yawn. Then came the opening of that fatal newspaper: it was war.

V

THE THIRD RUSSIA

MODERN Russia collapsed, whereas ancient Russia dissolved; yet the two events occurred in general conditions that are recognisably similar. On the one hand there were the builders of the nation, all too few of them; on the other there was almost the entire Russian people. It was thus when Peter the Great ascended the throne, and it was just the same when the last Tsar fell from it. The situation, it is true, was not utterly desperate; after all these centuries it was now about to change, was actually changing. Then came the war and it was all too late.

Neither the government, nor the majority of the élite that by contrast was called "society", was ever capable of absorbing the peasantry into the nation, of making it grasp the idea of national unity or national dignity. This was a task accomplished by the revolution, which swept away government and society alike, State along with culture, by destroying all that had been understood under the old régime as the nation. Of the various breaches of continuity that Russia has known, this was undoubtedly the most radical. The construction that was destroyed was not in itself without power or grandeur; all that had been lacking was a firm foundation. It had been the work of a minority—such a construction must always be—but a minority too aloof from the rest of the country. In 1917, this minority decided it would make a revolution; but upon this the people—the "land", as it was said—finally rose from its long sleep and from the formless state in which it had been left so long, to take its revenge on all that was other than the land. In the February of that year, the old Russian State, the Empire founded by Peter the Great, was shaken but still stood; in October it was prostrate, its ruins swamped by the rising tide of the people: the people that the revolution had now released, to give it a momentary illusion of freedom before making it submit to its own hard law.

FROM STATE WITHOUT PEOPLE TO PEOPLE WITHOUT STATE

When war broke out there were a number of patriotic demonstrations in Russia, all more or less compulsory, and they were followed, in the capitals, by popular commotions of very great violence. But there was also plenty of sincere enthusiasm; there was even a kind of armistice between government and opposition, between liberal Russia and official Russia. The nation, at any rate at first, seemed one; but, in spite of all the efforts of those latter years, the people themselves were still absent from the nation. They were mobilised and they obeyed; they went to the front; they fought with patience and courage. But all this meant nothing. Their heart was not in it; it was not their war.

In spite of Stolypin's uncompleted reforms, in spite of the recent changes in Russian life, the State was still something remote in the eyes of the peasants, something hostile and incomprehensible, existing merely to extort taxes and enforce military service; it was a foreign body, a usurping system superimposed on their life of immemorial custom. Both government and opposition belonged to a world about which they knew nothing at all. The propaganda of the old *intelligentsia*, and of the new, left them entirely cold, except for its promise of a speedy distribution of manorial lands. This was the one thing they had been hoping for, ever since their liberation in 1861; it was the only means they could conceive of escaping from their poverty and bettering their standard of life. This was all they had expected from the revolution of 1905; and as neither Tsar nor parliament had conceded their heart's desire they had lost faith in the one and hope in the other. What the liberal parties had obtained at that time, and what the government had reluctantly yielded to the opposition, was of interest to a relatively insignificant minority; it had no effect at all on the hundred and twenty-odd million peasants that made up

"Russia" in a very real sense, though not in the sense of the Russian State or even in that of the Russian nation.

The war proved this conclusively; it revealed the hidden disease that preyed on the great Empire, a total lack of cohesion and homogeneity. The peasants, turned soldiers and fighting at the front, had a patriotism that was merely provincial—for Tver or Toula—hardly any sense at all of a common fatherland. They were certainly aware of being Russians; but this meant language, religion and customs, and doubtless also the fact of their all being peasants; it had nothing whatever to do with the State or public life, and men who came from Tver could scarcely imagine they had interests in common with any of their fellows who came from Toula. As for conscripts from Siberia, from the Urals, or even from the centre of European Russia, they had no feeling at all of defending their own fields or homes and families; the front was too far away. Would even France have such a lively sense of moral unity if it were a fortnight's train-journey from Bordeaux to Lille? It was Russia's misfortune that the people had never learnt to take any real part in the life of the State; and that the State, as in the past, was quite incompetent to rouse or penetrate or organise the people, to make them understand their interests and realise that whereas the whole of Russia belonged to them they were themselves responsible for the whole of Russia. The peasant-soldier could endure the greatest fatigues and privations, he could obey and fight and if necessary die; but, once discipline was relaxed and constraint removed, he could not be expected to continue on his own a struggle of which the meaning had always been obscure to him.

Two and a half years of war had been all that was necessary to break the internal resistance of the Russian State; as for the country's non-bureaucratic élite, all the resources that "society" was in a position to command, in the way of moral authority or political energy, were exhausted by a mere eight months of revolution. When the Soviets seized power, the State —now only the cultured minority that had hitherto formed the nation—had to yield to a handful of skilful agitators, who knew very well how to use for their own ends the destructive energies accumulated in the people. Over the ruins of modern Russia, and implicitly of old Russia as well, the revolution could go its way to what was really its goal, the creation of a third Russia, even though that goal was wholly obscure to itself; and this, in spite of all its supposed ends, in spite of the ideologies in which it was decked, and over the heads of its leaders—even of his to whom it owed its success.

Lenin willed the revolution; he had realised that the war made it possible; he knew the means that must be employed to secure its triumph and also to prevent its halting half way. All the rest, the personal motives of the leader and his associates, their political convictions, and the Marxism they made less a system of ideas than a language (a language that has shown itself since to be capable of surviving the ideas)—all these things may be interesting in themselves, but their importance was no more than purely instrumental in regard to the great events that changed so profoundly the inner structure of the country. Lenin willed the revolution, the whole revolution, and nothing but the revolution. Others, carried to power by those events of the spring of 1917, wanted other things as well: they wanted to carry on the war, and more efficiently than under the Tsar; to win, if possible, Constantinople and the Straits; to fraternise with the western democracies; to endow Russia with a perfect political régime by means of a Constituent Assembly elected on principles of pure democracy, the principles laid down in the latest manuals of constitutional law. For such fine things as these, Lenin had hardly a thought. What he observed was that the country was breaking up of its own accord, and it was this that chiefly delighted him. His propaganda was primarily addressed to the soldiers, whom he invited to leave the front and return to their homes; to the peasants, whom he advised to partition the land without waiting for any permission from the government; to the workers and the demi-intellectuals, whose appetite he sharpened with a clever rehash of the Marxism of 1890, plus the nihilism of 1860. His slogans were taken from anywhere: "He who will not work must be left to starve", from St. Paul (as quoted, of course, by Marx); "Peace to the cottages, war to the mansions", this from the Jacobins; as for

"All power to the Soviets", that was something he owed to his own political instinct. To him, all means were good; he would stoop to any demagogic device, disdain no collaboration, no kind of collaborator. "The man who hesitates to soil his hands has no business in politics"—such was his declared principle. The famous Italian poet, seeking to raise the mob in Venice in 1798, received from the French consul the following advice: "My dear Monsieur Foscolo, to make a revolution you must have people to hang." Lenin was well aware how revolutions are made.

How rejoiced he must have been, at the end of that year, to see the people, now Stateless, storming the railway-trucks in order to return to Toula or Tver; massacring all who resisted them; burning the manor-houses, together with their owners, their old furniture and libraries; spitting out their hatred, so long pent up, against all who were not the people, against all who wore a jacket or collar and tie. Marxism, even in its Leninist form, had extremely little to do with all this. Russia was an agrarian, not an industrial country; its proletariat was not numerous and the revolution was not directed against capitalism or the middle class but against what was really the superstructure of the country, against all who in their clothes or their manner of life, in their taste or education, differed rather too widely from the mass of the people. The class-war doctrine is hardly an explanation of what happened in Russia; but it was an excellent ideology to serve as an incitement, to awaken what till then had merely lain dormant, to sharpen resentment against what was really lack of understanding rather than oppression, and to set a spark to the tinder that had been collecting for centuries. To exterminate the élite—the élite of every kind—would assure the final success of the revolution; Lenin received this guarantee at the hands of the Russian people.

In the revolution's first phase, the people's natural allies had been the host of demi-intellectuals reinforced by a fairly large number of workers, sharper or rather better educated than the rest. As time went on, communist doctrines did much to queer the pitch, for the makers of the revolution and also for their opponents, and when there was an attempt to apply them in the rural areas they inflicted on the peasants much unnecessary suffering. But in the early days Lenin used them in a purely opportunist fashion: it was not the triumph of communism he was after, it was the success of the revolution. To ensure its complete success he had to do more than overthrow the government, he had to destroy the whole State; and destroy it he did, or allowed it to be destroyed. To ensure that it should be done with no interference from the outside world it was necessary to sign the peace of Brest-Litovsk; this he did, without allowing himself to be influenced by the palavering of Trotsky, who favoured some sort of intermediate solution which was neither war nor peace. It could never be said of Lenin that the revolution carried him to power. It was he who carried the revolution; he made it, and he prevented it from being unmade; the rest was all a series of compromises, measures dictated *ad hoc* by circumstances, not without analogies in other periods of history when other rulers of Russia had used similar means.

THE COLLAPSE OF THE EMPIRE

The day after the assassination of Alexander II, Pobedonostsev, the procurator-general of the Holy Synod and a recognised mouthpiece of the monarchical extremists, declared war on the "constitutionalism" favoured by the minister Loris-Melikov, by proclaiming, among other things: "Russia is strong by virtue of her autocracy, by virtue of unlimited confidence, the mutual confidence between people and Tsar in such close association. It is an inestimable boon, this intimate communion of the Tsar with the people." This personage, it is well known, played an important part in the two following reigns as an inspirer of that "reaction" so hateful to liberal opinion and to the revolutionary parties. Primarily it was the desire to maintain the theocratic character of the Russian monarchy, as being the sole *mystique* of power that the people could understand, because it was something with which they had always been familiar. It was certainly doubtful, *a priori*, how anything like national unity could be realised as long as it was centred in a constitutional idea. And obviously, with a view to such unity, a close communion between Tsar and people could not fail to appear as an "inestimable boon". But did such a communion exist in fact? Had the people any real confidence in the Tsar? Did they even know him? Was not Samarin nearer the truth when he spoke of that *mystical* being on whom the people conferred a "quasi-divine majesty", but who was not identified in their minds with the Emperor as the executive head of the State? The government was mistaken rather less than the *intelligentsia* in the picture it formed of the Russian people, but it was mistaken all the same. The two last Tsars made very sincere attempts to recover the confidence of the people. But in doing so they showed a most pitiful ineptitude, and their mistakes, especially those of the two last, did irreparable damage to the prestige of the crown. All decent people were sick and tired of the new *Union of the Russian People* and its "black centuries", which organised pogroms with the connivance and sometimes the assistance of the police. People shrugged their shoulders at the numerous puerilities suggested to the imperial family by their mawkish pandering to popular sentiment, by all the talk at court about "our dear peasants", "our brave soldiers", and such expressions of boundless love for the faithful people of holy Russia. This tendency, in which a certain sincerity was mingled with something extremely forced and artificial, could only have results that were either sinister or absurd. Its last embodiment was Rasputin, a character that might have been invented by an artist of genius as a diabolical personification of all that was prodigiously false in the picture of his people formed by the unhappy Tsar.

Two tragic incidents were perfect symbols of this ridiculous misunderstanding, and they both foreshadowed the bloody end of the reign. The first was a mere accident, though it acquired all the significance of a very grim omen. At the Tsar's coronation in Moscow, a vast multitude thronged the Khodynski esplanade to catch a distant glimpse of the imperial couple and a share of the trifling gifts that were distributed. A mad rush ensued, some of the stands collapsed and the police on the spot were unable to prevent some thousands from being injured—visitors for the most part from outlying districts—and there were a thousand more who perished in the stampede. The impression created by the disaster was profound and lasting; the hopes inspired by the person of the young Tsar—ill-founded enough—darkened perceptibly after this. But the second event, that happened nine years later—the famous "Red Sunday" of 22 January 1905—had infinitely greater importance; it marked a decisive turning-point in the destiny of the Tsar and in that of his Empire.

This episode of the first revolution engraved itself the more deeply in the memory of the people because in this, as they had never been before, they were themselves directly involved. The strike that led up to it had spread among the workers of Petersburg, whose mentality was still much like that of the peasants, for they always tended to keep in touch with their native villages. The strikers were not led by the usual agitators but by a young priest, Gapon, a former prison-chaplain, who enjoyed the secret protection of the police and the Ministry of the Interior because the syndicalism he advocated aimed purely at social reform without any political demands that could endanger the government. Finding himself at the head of a movement that included a considerable number of workers, among whom he had acquired an enormous prestige, Gapon suggested making the Tsar directly acquainted with their grievances by presenting a formal petition. On Sunday, 22 January, there advanced towards the Winter Palace a procession of some twenty thousand workers, singing hymns as they went, and carrying ikons and portraits of the Tsar. The petition they were to offer demanded extensive reforms, both social and political, but it left untouched the principle of monarchy and the terms in which it was expressed were the humblest imaginable. The Tsar was warned, however, that if he failed to meet his people, about two o'clock, he would lose their confidence and risk severing the bonds between country and throne. This warning the Emperor declined to take seriously. He left for Tsarskoie-selo and the troops were called out. The procession, on arriving before the Palace, was ordered to disperse; when it failed to obey immediately, the troops opened fire. Several hundred workers were killed or wounded. Gapon, who had raised his crucifix and attempted to parley, was one of the first to fall, killed by a bullet. Rifle-fire and arrests continued until nightfall. So it became very difficult indeed, after Red Sunday, to speak of "unlimited mutual confidence" or of any "close communion" between the Tsar and the Russian people.

The square before the Palace is not very far from that before the Senate, and at an interval of eighty years volley answered volley. The people had not been present on the Senate Square; but they were present before the Palace, for the first and last time, with their priest and their ikons and the name of the Tsar on their lips; and there before them were their little brothers the soldiers—who shot them down. Presently, in the same symbolic and grandiose setting, there would be other shouts to be heard, other crowds to be seen. At the end of the winter, twelve years later, the streets were full of people. In front of the bakers' shops women were screaming for bread, and the few red flags that floated over the processions bore the slogans: "Down with autocracy!" "Down with the War!" Already soldiers were joining the demonstrators, for the revolt had also broken out in the capital's four main barracks: among them that of the Preobrajensky regiment of foot guards, the most famous in Russia and the first of those that formed the nucleus of Peter the Great's new army. The crowd invaded the parliament house, set fire to public buildings, stripped all officers of their badges of rank and killed a number of policemen who made a show of resistance. Already a parliamentary committee was set up to proceed with the formation of a provisional government. The Emperor abdicated in favour of his younger brother, who in turn renounced the throne. Whereupon the throne remained vacant. The revolution took its place. And it intended to reign—in spite of the good folk who failed to understand why it lingered in power, now that it had done all it was expected to accomplish.

It reigned. It reigned for years before it ever governed, before it understood what government meant. The game was played, the war was lost, a shameful peace was duly concluded; there was no more Emperor, no more Empire; the imperial family had been done to death like a litter of puppies. Now famine raged and civil war was at its height. Yet people lived less in the present than in the past; or rather they lived outside time altogether, surrounded by traces of splendour now for ever out of reach, never more to be used. Russia was no longer. It is easy to be reconciled to what is dead. St. Petersburg had not yet changed its name; the churches in Moscow remained open. People in the street were still allowed to say what they thought. Those who were actually there, in those terrible years when Russia was changing her soul, remember the strange kind of tragic enthusiasm in the air, something that made the heart beat faster, gave a new relish to life. A huge building had collapsed; it was possible to walk among its ruins, admiring their magnificence and also the force of the shock that had so suddenly created them. Authority was on holiday, or else stark mad; it provided you with no food, it might sometimes make a direct attempt upon your life; but it no longer compelled you to earn your daily bread, to rise at a particular time, to do this or that, to feel responsible for what might happen either to you or yours. There triumphed during this brief interlude, as never before, that subtly anarchical instinct of the Russian people, the instinct that Pugatchev and Razin had turned to account. All that the revolution could give in the way of poetry and inspiration, it exhausted in the course of these few strange years.

It is true that from the outset, side by side with the enthusiasm and the tragedy, of which you were at once the victim and the spectator, there was also an element of constraint and regimentation. But it was all so inefficient! The first government machinery to be organised with any success was that of the political police; but even this, at the beginning, did its massacring haphazard; it allowed many to escape whom it would have liked to kill twice, and it was some considerable time before it became worthy of its chief, the impeccable Comrade Dzerjinski. For the rest it was all regulations, pedantic and pettifogging, mingled with a clownish, unbelievable, and almost endearing confusion. An impotent bureaucracy is a sorry sight, but one not wholly unpleasing to Russian eyes. The whole country was a vastly magnified version of the "Commission of Surveillance of the Commission of Control", that a character of Gogol's established in his domain. Moreover the government was too busy to undertake, as yet, the systematic stifling of the spiritual life. The universities, the museums, the artistic, literary or learned societies, were all so many peaceful oases, where though cheek by jowl with death, and always menaced by lack of food or the vigilance of the party, you still felt free to discuss and to think, to cultivate the things of the spirit, to read (or not to read) the complete works of Marx and his devoted friend Engels. The peasants themselves were haunted by hunger; but meanwhile they could enjoy bartering a sack of flour for a suite of furniture, all gilded and flowery, or for a silent but monumentally impressive piano; while their daughters learnt to make up their faces and their sons to use the right revolutionary jargon.

That was the time to see the Palmyra of the North in the majestic misery that endowed it with a new beauty: its suddenly yawning squares, its distances subtly merging into haze; its main streets all silent after the noisy tumults of war and insurrection, forgetful of the familiar sounds of the time gone by when the city was still alive; its stations now without trains, its port without ships, the palaces along the quays all staring blindly; the Stock Exchange, on the other side of the river, again a temple, and there was the Smolny convent, all whirls and spirals, entablatures and rock-work, Rastrelli's astonishing currant-and-cream cake, royally served on a vast platter of snow, which in the days of October had been the revolutionary headquarters. During the yellow thaw, at the end of 1920, there were few people to be met in the centre of the city; these walked in the middle of the street, the houses on either side being riddled with bullets, revealing their nudity through crumbling plaster and the planks that served as a dressing for their wounded windows and plate-glass. People passed under the triumphal arch and then seemed to lose themselves, adrift in the great square; at the far side of it the Winter Palace, in that livid light in which the city slept, seemed merely its own shadow, haunted by the ghosts of those who had once dwelt in it. But far into the night, and into the fate there was no escaping, the city preserved her own spectral beauty, looking fairer than ever in the washed air of spring, untarnished by smoke from the now silent factories, her porticos and colonnades displaying once again the graces no longer enjoyed, no longer of this world.

The city was still there, but there was already a feeling that you were walking among its ruins. You were alive and free; equally ready either to live or to die. The simple things were appreciated more than ever: the infinite worth of a glass of water or a piece of bread. Death had come; and lo, you were still alive! It was possible to walk, though a little falteringly, in the keen wind of the future. All about was desert, even as had been foretold; but the Bronze Horseman still held his arm outstretched over all that now had become once more his dream. Then not only the stones of the great city, and its waters, but Russia herself, as she had existed for two centuries in her splendour and misery, now for ever ended, became something as fleeting and as irrevocably lost as one of those sudden northern lights, brightening and then fading in Petersburg's wintry sky.

THE REVOLUTION ENTHRONED

Every revolution is a mixture of two elements, wholly different in kind. One is to be found in any revolt or insurrection, whereas the other only in what is strictly a revolution, a comparatively new phenomenon in modern Europe. Symbols of the first are the taking of the Bastille, the Marseillaise, Valmy; of the second, the division of France into departments, the adoption of the metric system, the regular and assiduous functioning of the guillotine. They can be called respectively the riot-element and the system-element. The first was strong in Russia as long as the civil war lasted; it persisted all through the terror and the famine right down to the establishment of the New Economic Policy, and to some extent even to the death of Lenin (in January 1924). The other was never in the ascendant till later, though implicitly it was contained in the first and could be deduced from it as the second of the two stages: rational destruction and "socialist construction". In the Russian revolution, the contrast between these two elements and the complexity of their mutual opposition make up the whole of the strictly revolutionary phase.

An expert player of *pelote basque* can hardly be expected to be first class at bowls. Lenin was a revolutionary, he was not a statesman. For him, the first thing was to destroy the State in order to make the revolution; afterwards the State had to be reconstructed to preserve the revolution. Here, as a strategist and tactician he has scarcely his equal, either in Russia or anywhere else; the reason being that he combined an extreme elasticity in theory and practice with an unparalleled power of concentrating on the one end, which was (to use the favourite expression of Russian lawyers and policemen) "subversion of the established order". It was this order he hated, with a hatred that was not in the least romantic: it was a controlled hatred, clear-sighted and all-embracing. Every established order had to be overthrown, both in Russia and the entire world. Revolution itself was an absolute: the final end and the supreme good. These two formulas, the vast content of which he had rather felt than thought, might explain well enough the initial impulse of the Russian revolution. Lenin had many features in common with the intellectuals of the old school: his lay asceticism, the simplicity of his tastes, the prolixity of his style. He had also a strong personality of his own. But his work overshadowed it; he would have been nothing at all if he had had nothing to destroy. Yet, if it was to be successful, this very destruction demanded more than audacity; it demanded prudence as well. The paradox of any lasting revolution is the need it has to be preserved and consolidated. Lenin's famous trimming, branded by some as treason, was only a measure of preservation: not the preservation of the people, the nation or its culture, but of the one thing dear to him, revolution itself. And, in spite of fears to the contrary, it was not the system-element that suffered by it; it was the riot-element that was to crawl away and die.

Opinion in the West is generally much mistaken about the
N.E.P. and the changes it effected in the course of the Russian
revolution. The temporary return, and it was only a partial
one, to a liberal "bourgeois" régime in commerce and industry
obviously brought immediate and very considerable relief in
all that concerned material conditions; but to the spiritual life
of Russia it was nothing short of disastrous, because once relieved from preoccupation with famine and civil war, the
government had leisure to turn its attention to this, and with
cold deliberation to exterminate it utterly. In the early days it
had allowed intelligence and imagination to have more or less
free play in their own particular spheres: these were still independent of political directives or economic considerations.
On any but political issues, opinion was virtually as free as it
was in Hitler's Germany. Teaching in the university generally
escaped the surveillance of the party, so that it was possible to
discuss the Odyssey or the Sistine Chapel without having to
drag in the subject of the class-war. Artists produced their
works, writers wrote and published their writings, without
being liable to be called on to produce an insurance policy
taken out with the firm of Marx, Engels & Co. But all that was
soon changed: it was untidy and intolerable. It was during this
transitional period—from 1921 to 1924—that the majority of
writers and artists, most, in fact, who had any high degree of
culture, left their native land to become émigrés. Thenceforward the vice that imprisoned the life of the spirit closed more
and more tightly. The last comparatively independent review,
The Russian Contemporary, founded by Gorki in 1923, failed to
survive to 1924. In 1925 it would have been impossible to publish books that had appeared with impunity two or three years
before. The radical reform of higher education, carried out by
Pokrovski in 1924, transformed the universities into Marxist
institutes; all the subjects taught in them, from mathematics to
the history of art, had to be regarded as applications of dialec-
tical materialism, or else as auxiliary sciences subordinate to it.
There was a remorseless expulsion of students who were unable
to prove satisfactorily that they were of strictly peasant or proletarian descent. The watchful control of artistic and intellectual

life became one of the chief tasks of the government and the party. Here, at any rate, there was nothing to fear from famine or armed force. Thus the State could safely return and wring liberty's neck.

The anarchy of those first revolutionary years was clearly something that would pass; the State had to come back; riot must yield to system. Those who controlled the government during Lenin's illness and after his death acted partly under the influence of his doctrine—it was the only one they knew— and partly under pressure of circumstances; for, after riot and system, revolution tends invariably to end in compromise. Like their most vigorous predecessors in other periods of history, these masters of the third Russia endeavoured primarily to keep the vast country under control, and as long as they were in power to impose on it a uniform regimentation; rigid, it is true, and inhuman in detail, but on the whole efficient. Thus their organisation of foreign trade was very similar to the Tsar Peter's; in rural economy, their policy was reminiscent of some of the measures of the formidable Arakcheev, the reactionary minister of Alexander I; the function of the party and the political police suggested that of the *oprichnina* under Ivan the Terrible; and the "specialists", the "stakhanovists", the Red Army officers, and the "capabilities" of the *komsomol*—what are these but the "nobility of service" of Peter the Great's régime? From the time when the party passed from destruction to construction, from the time, that is, when it began to govern effectively, its governmental activity proved intenser and far more penetrating than that of all the best riders that had ever ridden the Russian mare, not even excluding the Bronze Horseman himself. They could never, it is true, get rid of theories that were wholly inapplicable to practice; but in spite of this they got nearer to their objectives; and the reason was that, thanks to the revolution, they were dealing with a country that was more united and homogeneous; they were not limited, either, in their choice of means by any moral considerations, by force of custom, or by any respect for the value of the individual or human life. Undoubtedly the Soviet State is the most powerful that has ever existed on Russian soil; it is one in which the rulers for the first time have had a grip on the whole country, have been able to impose on it their slightest wish and receive in return not only passive obedience but an activity which they are able to employ as they will, without being accountable to anyone—save to the chief of chiefs. He, whatever the post he occupies officially, and whether he calls himself the secretary of the party, father of the peoples, generalissimo or comrade, is a sovereign more absolute than was ever the Tsar. It was with him, on his invisible throne, that the revolution was accomplished.

Swift, writing in 1701, observes that peoples in insurrection work only for their own destruction and the benefit of some tyrant, "with as blind an instinct as those worms that die with weaving magnificent habits for beings of a superior order to their own". "The land of the workers" to-day, according to the official doctrine, knows nothing of the exploitation of labour, of any conflict between a governed and a governing class; yet it is clear enough that a new governing class is in process of formation, and that in the interest of this class the State, in Russia, is exploiting the workers, more proletarian than ever before, by all kinds of means, some long since repudiated by the capitalist world. But the beings of a superior nature refrain (at least in public) from wearing habits that are too magnificent; and the official lie contains one grain of truth, because the exploited worker submits to his lot much more readily if he can be made to believe it is common to all, if he can be persuaded that the forced-labour enterprise called the State belongs as much to him as to any of his comrades. Enough of them will believe it, as long as the ruling class is not unduly distinguished from the rest, in outward appearance, in education and basic tastes, and in the values recognised on one side and the other. In spite of all that the economists try to persuade us, inequality of fortune (and inequality of power) can be carried off better that inequality of culture. This, among other things, explains why the class struggle in the United States is of a relatively benign character; oppressors and oppressed are more like one another than they are in the Old World, though less so than they are in the very new world of the U.S.S.R. So there is some advantage in having a ruling class that is not too highly cultured: a fact seemingly realised by the demagogues and dictators of modern times. The *Kulturabbau*, as it was recently called in Germany, has its points. This once achieved, it is possible for all to be pals together; everyone talks the same slang; every privileged position being recently acquired, none looks inaccessible. In this way the governing class, arousing less hatred, has so much the better opportunity to cheat. The silkworms die in the consoling belief that they are at any rate weaving clothes for their own posterity.

From the point of view of Russian history, the two main achievements of the revolution were these: the unifying of the country by making it more homogeneous than it had ever been in the past; the creation of a new governing class, less separated than the old from the mass of the people. Such changes in a country's destiny are of incalculable importance; they mark the end of an era and they dominate the future. One Russia was dead, another had been born; only this other is hidden from us: we can never see it, we can hardly guess what it is; all we see is the scaffolding, formerly used by the revolution and now serving to support its throne. The new man is indistinguishable from the propaganda sandwich-man; every human voice is drowned by the roaring of the indefatigable loud-speaker. For Russia the revolution has opened vast possibilities: the revolution enthroned takes care they are never realised.

THE EURASIAN EMPIRE

Lenin had good reason for not taking too hardly the terms of peace imposed on him by Germany; he probably foresaw that things would move speedily in this century of speed. It needed only a quarter of it for Brest-Litovsk to be forgotten at Potsdam; for the unfledged Leviathan (mistaken for a colossus with feet of clay), conquered by the Poles and hounded out of the Baltic, to be able to swallow up the Baltic, together with Poland and Bessarabia as well, the latter seasoned with the rest of Rumania. What the newspapers had taken to be Russia's disappearance (relatively speaking) from history, proved to be no more than a theatrical exit; the State that had absented itself duly returned; the Empire that had foundered was rebuilt on new foundations. Neither its architecture nor its basic idea was that of the old. Indeed there is a curious contrast between the architecture and the idea, for though the new Empire is federal in form its content is authoritarian; its passions are nationalist, its pretensions international. Why these contradictions? For the simple reason that they are its most useful assets and the truest guarantees of its power. The surest centralisation is that which preserves the appearances of autonomy. Annexation succeeds better when it looks like voluntary adhesion. The return to tax-paying was accepted lightly enough when compulsion to pay was disguised as a benevolence. Elections go well when the elector has no choice and dares not abstain. The most useful constitution in the world is a constitution that is never used. Such are some of the wise maxims that have made for the greatness of the new Empire. Here it was, extending its sceptre and its standards over all that vast space that had been once called Russia; preaching *das Kapital* to the Tchukchi and the Kirghiz; peopling the Polar Circle with corpses and with pioneers confined there behind barbed wire; hiding factories in the depths of Asia; already encroaching on the West, getting a grip on the Balkans, dominating Prague and Budapest, present in Vienna and Berlin. There are some who will say: "But don't you recognise the same 'great power' that was already formidable in the past, pursuing the same ends, remembering its former methods of attaining them, now playing the same cards, making use (as it always did) of ethnical relationships or religious affinities? Isn't this victorious Empire, so ambitious and so distrustful, just Russia once again, the Russia of Iermak and Potemkin, of Kunersdorf, Leipzig and Navarino?" The reply is that we only half recognise it as such.

True, geography has not changed, nor the policy (internal and external) that it determines. But can it be said that this was always the sole determining factor? Have not the judgments or prejudices of a particular age always played some part in things as well? Of course they have. That is why M. de Norpois would be wrong to identify the policy of the Kremlin with that of the Singers' Bridge. The latter, even in its most "realist" proceedings, never lost sight of the traditional picture of Europe and Christendom, never denied the values represented by Western Europe, and never failed to remember Russia's moral prestige as a sister-nation to the nations of Europe. The new Empire, willing as it is to use the body of the old, utterly rejects its spirit. Europe is nothing to it, Christianity an absurd relic, and the values of the West a mere debased currency. If it takes thought for its prestige, it is in terms of industrial power and propaganda—in the effectiveness, that is, of a certain set of lies. The very name it so laboriously constructed for itself is simply a piece of publicity. In its essence it is anonymous: universal, to a degree never known till our day. In its own eyes it is itself the true "middle Empire": the centre of the world, with a vocation to extend to the world's periphery; a prophetic image of the whole of humanity unified and ruled. In the eyes of others, it may either be this or something else; those who call it Russia through sheer force of habit should really refer to it as the Eurasian Empire.

This name has come to fit it, not because of the territory it has occupied without altering, but because it has deliberately played down its connection with Europe—the part it had in Europe during the Empire of the Tsars—in comparison with all it has in common with Asia. This is not a question of policy, which has been able, according to circumstances, and may still be able, to concentrate on any point either in the East or in the West; it is a question of initial choice and innate leaning. A thousand years ago the Slav people in Eurasia seem to have chosen for themselves a European destiny. The new Empire declares for Europe no more than for Asia. Actually it chooses neither. It leans to neither one side nor the other; feels no need to adhere to anything at all. And it could hardly be otherwise, for it is first and foremost, and in virtue of its very idea, a force of attraction and a centre of influence. It is everywhere and nowhere: Asiatic and European—Polynesian, if the occasion offers. It invites all peoples simply to knock at the door and it will open to them whatever their country of origin. The old quarrel, that so long divided Russian intellectuals, henceforth becomes pointless. Westernisers and slavophils have nothing to do but become reconciled, the more so—and here is the paradox of the situation—in that the extremists on both sides have seen their dearest aspirations all realised in a flash, at the expense of the moderates who once seemed more likely to reconcile both.

The intransigent westerniser, for whom western civilisation is simply the sum of various technical and scientific "conquests", rejoices chiefly at the absence in the Eurasian Empire of all those obstacles to the "victorious march of progress", the persistence of which obstacles he so much deplored in pre-Soviet Russia. The Church, whether persecuted or not, is without influence; the power, though still monarchical, is no longer trammelled by tradition. The new ruling class, in contrast to the old, is active, jealous of its privileges, greedy for gain, indifferent to the past, eager for the future. The condition of the peasant has grown closer to that of the worker; both are State proletarians; both go to their clubs, read the newspapers, listen to their masters' broadcasts, and by such means are made aware how happy they really are. They accept cheerfully enough the few shadows in the picture: ubiquitous police agents, informers, deportations; but now that they are once and for all on the progressive road, things like these must soon disappear. This surely was the cause upheld with their dying breath by the great standard-bearers of the West, the official defenders of humanitarianism and progress, men like H. G. Wells and Romain Rolland, never at all embarrassed by the little inconveniences of the régime or discredited intellectually by any blunders of their own. And above all what is really beautiful and unique in the country is that, with all its chauvinism, there is less and less talk of the nation and national peculiarities—considerations always so hateful to the westerniser. Besides, all superiority supposes a common standard. This Empire eagerly preaches to its faithful that they should pretend themselves superior while ignoring that they are different.

As for the slavophil, he is no less pleased at what he naturally sees from a rather different angle. Even if he is not greatly taken with some of the pan-Slav excrescences of the Eurasian policy, and if the official brand of patriotism in the U.S.S.R. is not wholly to his liking, he observes with delight that the capital is once more Moscow, not the city that had always filled him with such shame, the hybrid artificial Petersburg; that Russians no longer look abroad, and are constantly invited by their government to extol the beauties of the Caucasus and Siberia; that the literary, artistic and intellectual values that are quoted on 'change in London and Paris, are priced very low in the Kremlin, indeed not quoted at all; that the Russian people are daily taught, on the highest authority, to be content with their own true cultural legacy, duly expurgated by the approved executors of the will (working under the eyes of the police), and to ask nothing of a West that is utterly polluted—more so, apparently, than even the slavophil himself had ever imagined. This new Russia, he will declare, is like the old Muscovy: she is distrustful of the foreigner; she closes her frontiers; shuts herself up, depends on none but herself; it is thus she must grow, protected from harmful interference from without, and so in due course become exclusively Russian. "Excuse me," will doubtless retort one of his émigré disciples, "not Russian, Eurasian!" For that ideology too has something to rejoice at: it had got hold of a word, deduced from it an idea, turned this into a theory—and behold, here the very thing itself is offered to it on a plate!

In actual fact, the official uniform that right-thinking minds must adopt in sovietised Eurasia is a kind of chauvinist universalism. No garment could be more colourless; none more neutral or more indistinctive. For nationalism, however dangerous it may be, has a different shade of meaning in every different country, whereas chauvinism is completely without national flavour. In the advertising formula, dear to some firms of outfitters, it has been "made to measure in advance". The cloth, of very indifferent quality, comes wholly from the West. The Russian tailor, having taken his tradesman's course in the army, has cut out a khaki greatcoat, not very elegant but certainly sewn together, and to measure: "our" measure for all,

the *same* measure for all. It is not obligatory wear, except in
Eurasia; but for that matter it could be worn equally well in
the antipodes, and for all we know it may be familiar there
already. For even in the free countries it is being widely worn,
sometimes as a working garment, sometimes as evening dress.
Those who are behind the undertaking have spared no expense
in advertising and publicity. It is easier to wear than get
rid of. You like it? Take it, it's yours. Certainly it has no
resemblance to anything worn in Russia in the old days, or
in other countries of Europe—no resemblance, that is, to anything people wear when they dress to please themselves. The
Russia of yesterday, open to the West, resembled no one but
herself; the U.S.S.R., while it shrivels into itself, wears a propa-
gandist mask, impersonal and universal, thereby hoping the
better to resemble everyone else. For in its own eyes the only
things of any importance are the industrial and technical
achievements of the West—things that would interest India or
Japan just as much. Russia was a nation distinct from other
nations, but participating with them in a European unity;
the Eurasian Empire—more westernised, in one sense, than the
Empire of Peter the Great and Pushkin, yet more closed to
the West than the Muscovy visited by Olearius and Herber-
stein—is drawing daily further away from what Russia was
once and from what Europe is still.

ANTI-CULTURE

The destiny of the country that has undergone a revolution
depends primarily on the particular nature of the compromise
that the revolution, sooner or later, must make with reality.
To have any hope of enduring it must sacrifice something;
therefore the compromise must be made at the expense of an
ideology or of the external power of the State; at the expense
of the living standard (or even the life itself) of the citizens, or
else at the expense of their liberty and their culture. In Russia,
the Marxist ideology was transformed into a kind of sacred
language, the ritual usage of which it was important to know,
without attempting (a thing that would be extremely dan-

gerous) to be too particular about its exact signification. But eventually, in this form, it was firmly established; and foreign policy (as the Kremlin understands it) could hardly be carried on satisfactorily without it. The power of the State, at first destroyed, then for long very feeble, is now completely restored and far greater, internally and externally, than it was before. In the meantime several strata of society had been exterminated and the vast majority of the population reduced to misery. The misery continues; so does the process of extermination, all the more because it furthers the "concentrationary" sector of the Soviet's economic front; yet no one could state with perfect conviction that these things will always be inseparable from the régime, that they are part and parcel of its inner nature. But what really is of its nature is the stifling of the spiritual life in all its expressions. In the first instance, it was at the expense of freedom and culture that the revolutionary compromise was concluded in Russia.

Millions of human lives were sacrificed. Statisticians, of course, assure us that they hardly count at all in relation to the total population. But with all due respect to figures and statisticians, the life of the spirit is not a matter of figures, and personal values are not to be eliminated thus. A spiritual inheritance, once it is rejected, can be restored only by the few, supported by the good will of all; no material necessity demands such a restoration. If you squeeze the peasant, you can always unsqueeze him in the event of a bad harvest. Under compulsion of famine, Lenin authorised trading in 1921; but nothing could compel him to authorise culture, to grant an adequate field for everyone's free and spontaneous creation. Similarly his successor, having to prepare for war and afterwards win it, began in 1934 to authorise patriotism; later he encouraged it by all means in his power (including the worst), and ended by inaugurating, in 1943, what might be called a "New Ecclesiastical Policy". But could he agree to dissociating love of country from love of party, or allow the Church to speak in the name of the Christian conscience? The Spirit blows not where it wills under a totalitarian régime, and as culture is not considered a political priority, we still await in vain an authorisation that is not, and will never be, imposed on a government by any kind of political interest or calculation.

Deprived as she is by her masters of a true, which means a disinterested culture, Russia is not suffering from a simple lack; she appears before the world not just with empty hands (which would undoubtedly be preferable) : she offers the world a substitute by no means unknown to it, but one that nowhere else had ever reached so high a degree of saturation. It is what may rightly be described as an anti-culture. This, in its essence, is simply the systematic denial of every non-utilitarian value. It is what the Russian communists inherited from their forebears, the nihilists of 1860. They began to put it in practice not quite as soon as they could, but as soon as they had yielded (unwillingly) to Marxist orthodoxy, as soon as they had strangled revolt and consolidated the system. Once the revolution had set foot on the first step of the throne, it set its face against anarchy by stifling the last vestiges of freedom, subjecting the country's intellectual life to a régime that dried it up at its source, attacking ferociously all independent thought and enslaving all literature and art to its own ends. It was thus that anti-culture came to be installed. For those who propagate it, nothing exists but the usable and the measurable; nothing but brute matter, the force of numbers, and the addition of effort to gain greater efficiency. All spontaneity is an object of suspicion; contemplation is forbidden as passive resistance; quality must always give place to quantity; the only creativeness admitted is in the form of technical and scientific invention, compulsorily, of course, in the service of the State and the party. The only value of art or letters is the power they may have to help maintain the enthroned revolution and to further its future prosperity. What are more useful than the rest are the physical sciences and mathematics, which is one of the reasons for the privileged position they enjoy in the U.S.S.R. Another is because it is dangerous to tinker with the integral calculus; but it is wholly commendable, and even necessary, to falsify (in the same interest) certain awkward facts of history. A third reason might be said to belong to the religious order, for the sciences that further technical progress are the object of the same worship as technical progress itself, and technolatry is essentially the religion of anti-culture. So much so that the Soviet young, taught to worship mechanisation and industrial efficiency, may be in danger of substituting one idol for another, and when they recite their ritual prayers to Marx and Lenin it may well be it is to the god Ford they are really addressing them.

The first thirty years of the Third Russia may be considered as a period of conflict between culture and anti-culture; an unequal struggle if ever there was one, for though nothing is more powerful than the spirit when it is reverenced, when it is not there is nothing so easy to hunt down and expeditiously despatch. If things remain as they are now, its fate is a foregone conclusion. When the struggle began there were writers and artists in Russia whose work was still alive; there were literary and artistic schools; there were universities that could compare with those of the West. There were individuals, even among communists, who could speak without the use of stereotyped phrases, and there were a few people, everywhere, who still thought honestly. Not much of this is left now. Not quite all is exterminated; but the excitement, sometimes painful, of the revolution's first years has long since given place to a dismal monotony, a stagnation in which platitude and mediocrity reign supreme. Thought is prohibited; for it is a prohibition of thought to permit it to exist only in a casuistic form in which all the principles are known in advance. Religious life is not extinct, but ignorance of religion, imposed by the State on the whole younger generation, is such that if Russia is ever again to become a Christian country it will only be as the result of a new conversion. All human and historical knowledge has been forced into an ideological strait-jacket; even biology has had orders to conform to the strictest and most rigid Darwinism—no doubt because Darwin was a contemporary of Marx. In literature, vague humanitarian reminiscences are being submerged under a flood of regimented production: all standardised stuff, compulsorily tendentious and full of sham exaltation, inviting all and sundry, in the tones of a street-hawker, to die for the revolution (or industry, or country), and exhibiting on every occasion such poverty of expression, of imagination and thought as has rarely been witnessed in the history of letters. In the arts, there is an even more obvious return to the philistine splendours of the last century; the Russian counterparts to Roll and Gervex are again all the rage; "socialist realism" is distinguishable only by the subjects it treats from the anecdotal realism so beloved by Victorian shopkeepers and by the grocers of the Third Republic. As for the architecture, it is again neo-classical, imitating the imitation of an imitation, yet striving to be monumental—much like that so much revered by those two great admirers of architectual magnificence who until recently lived in Germany and Italy respectively.

But if architecture, like the arts of the theatre, is grandiloquent, tending naturally to the dictatorial in tone, it has shyly withdrawn from those earlier experiments, "constructivist" and other, indulged in during the first few years of the revolution, to take refuge in the bosom of that most bourgeois of all centuries—the nineteenth. The whole of literature and art is on its way back, beyond the period of the interrupted renewal, to 1860 or 1870: not to rejoin, most certainly, the few great isolated geniuses of that period, but to follow more closely the lessons taught by their younger contemporaries, by Pissarev and Tkatchev, who vented their sarcasm and abuse on those geniuses. From the anti-cultural point of view the retreat is an advance; it tends to stimulate a Prudhommesque platitude of form and a political didacticism of content, and the blend of these two makes the ideal kind of atmosphere for such a civilisation. It provides the means for an intensive stuffing of empty heads, while flattering what is feeblest in popular taste: its inability to resist whatever is worst and most bourgeois. Such flattery is useful: it makes it possible, after finally suppressing the high culture, to proceed with the suppression of the horizontal as well, hateful as it is for its ancient moral and religious foundations. There is a pretence, it is true, of preserving it in the form of folklore—songs, dances, regional costumes and the rest—but this is no more than the stuffing of the body after extinguishing its life. There is also a pretence of replacing it, and naturally with something more useful and solid: the multiplication table, the Marxist catechism for all, and the diffusion of the classics. As if it were quite unknown for a schoolboy to learn his verses by heart without having the slightest idea what they mean, or for a lover of light reading to appreciate Balzac simply for the things he has in common with Ponson du Terrail. In itself, admittedly, it is not a bad thing to go to school, and the reading of Pushkin and Tolstoy may show up the worthlessness of what is being written at the present day; but the sum total of these efforts (in so far as they are not actually destructive) has only one lesson to teach us at present: namely that the totally illiterate may have more genuine culture than the mere readers of newspapers, and that compulsory education is by no means incompatible with a perfectly authentic barbarism.

The real problem for Russia, thirty years after the revolution, is not primarily political: it is the problem of her spiritual existence, and *therefore* of the régime that can make her spiritual existence again possible. Communism as a social doctrine has nothing to do with it; it is only the word, in any case, that exists in Eurasia, not the thing itself. What really matters is rationalist obscurantism which the Russian communists, having inherited it from the nihilists, have imposed on their own country and are attempting to impose on the world. (All this, after all, so deeply foreign to the old Russia, is really of western origin, and there would seem to be nothing to prevent its being exported *en masse*.) As long as this remains the basis of Soviet education, of Soviet *Weltanschauung*, there will be no culture in Russia, and the culture of other countries will also be threatened. For any people at all, culture is not something impersonal, an interchangeable sum total of knowledge and aptitudes; it is a people's very soul, manifested in its whole creative existence. It is this soul, rather than the body, that is to-day imperilled for all peoples. Her own, half lost, Russia alone can save.

After a desperate struggle and infinite suffering the Russians succeeded in winning their war. If peace continues it will make possible a rise in their material standards. As for the spiritual nourishment that only freedom can make accessible, if they are unable to break their chains their hunger will remain unsatisfied. Of two things one: either Russia will cease to be herself, lose every authentic link with her past and turn away for good from her former thinkers, writers and artists, to become what America might be without freedom, without communion with Europe, without her continuity of Anglo-Saxon civilisation; or else she will again find her soul, however much changed, recognise herself once more in her past, and finally reject, not the inalienable part of what she has received from the revolution—not even the doctrine, disintegrating already of its own accord and now only a bait for foreign consumption—but the whole of anti-culture itself, which must inevitably, in that event, give place to culture.

VI

THE RUSSIAN SOUL

THE title of this section is so like that unfortunate expression "The Slav Soul"—a crossroads of incurable and age-long misunderstandings—that there is a strong temptation to put it also in inverted commas. However, there is probably no other that could express any better the common substratum of a great many Russian ideas, Russian things and ways of life. A people's soul is unknowable till it has created a culture, a system of forms that may be said to be the incarnation of its soul; but it is enough to have tasted some of the fruits of that culture to be tempted to describe and explain it, to demonstrate exactly what it is which that culture embodies, even though it be just as impossible here to separate form and content as it would be with a work of art or a human life. That is why any attempt of this kind, however necessarily incomplete, subjective and one-sided, can be justified quite as much as a biographical study, the analysis of a picture or the appreciation of a tragedy.

The broad judgments finally passed on such a subject are nearly always summary and very often false, but it is more reasonable to think it possible to correct some of these judgments than to hope to refrain from judging altogether. From even the hastiest generalisation, provided it is not too superficial, it is possible to extract at least a grain of truth; and hatred, just like love, can go with much clear-sightedness. The Marquis de Custine, whose visit dates back to 1839, and the Baltic German, Victor Hehn, who lived in Petersburg for many years under Alexander II, were both of them obviously unjust to Russia, but this by no means obscured their vision and Hehn, who hated her intensely, showed that as an observer he was singularly perspicacious.[1] Some fifteen years ago the

---

[1] In the following pages I make extensive use of one of his too little known books, *De Moribus Ruthenorum* (Stuttgart, 1892). The papers collected in this posthumous

late Jules Legras published a work on Russia, very well documented, in which he turned to account even the most casual and absurd observations made by visitors in the course of the last four centuries. Nor can a Russian afford to ignore the opinion of foreigners; knowing his country from the inside, by way of introspection, he can appreciate all the better the difficulty there is in expressing such knowledge. To him "the Russian soul", a somewhat redundant term, sounds more objectionable than it does to another, seeing that what is referred to is really his own soul, in so far as it is associated with that of his country; and to the soul of his country nine full centuries went to the making, before events occurred that, for all one knows, may very well have given her a new one.

THE FAMILY CONNECTION

Jordaens' *Family Portrait* in the Hermitage Gallery always seemed to me to have a secret affinity with something specially Russian. In this picture, as in all the painter's work, there is a lively sense of the human nest, that close community in which all its members are plunged, as it were, seeming to bathe in the mysterious fluid that emanates from it. When he paints a gay festivity, as he often does, the guests seem always to be poor but snug; they fill the frame by themselves, with little room for accessories; they seem to be living a common life, in communion with a single soul; one ends where the other begins, the second always appearing to be a continuation of the first, without anything very much to distinguish or separate him. When the painter is dealing with a family in the strict sense, the child gives the impression of being really a continuation of its parents' lives; the brothers and sisters are so many shoots from the same branch; a particular forebear has his roots in the earth itself, where he merges into the subterranean life of his whole line. It is just this sense of family bonds, of the visceral warmth enveloping the life of the household, that is something very Russian; or perhaps something very old, better preserved in

---

volume go back to the years 1857-73. Hehn is also known as the author of excellent books that have nothing to do with Russia or the Russians.

Russia than anywhere else. The literature of the country provides numerous examples of it, and among its great writers the one who represented this instinct most powerfully was Tolstoy. That may be the reason why he is the most Russian of Russian geniuses.

Tolstoy's life, as much as his work, bears witness to this characteristic. This is clear from the memoirs of his daughter Alexandra, in which Tolstoy and his wife, like tutelary deities, preside afar or close at hand over the lives of those simple mortals, their children, their servants or their guests. As they grew up and married, the children never became detached from the family, or if they did so externally, not in ties of blood, in their collective memory and in all the profoundest elements of their lives; their joys and sorrows, their respective destinies and personal loves, might separate but could never divide them. The strength of the bonds that united Tolstoy to his wife and children are revealed in many of the details and incidents recorded by Alexandra Lvovna. It is apparent in the way he participated, with sympathy or hostility but always wholeheartedly, in the loves and married lives of his sons and daughters; so too in the painful keenness with which he felt to the very end whatever had reference to his relations with his wife. It may even be conjectured that his going away at eighty-two, which was to end in his death, is not to be explained by a simple desire to be free from an environment that hampered his living a life in conformity with his teaching, but rather by a craving to escape from himself, to flee that instinct for the *gens* always so deep in him, conflicting as it did with his rational theorising and moral consciousness that had no use for instinct and never ceased to combat it, though never succeeding in subduing it completely.

Tolstoy's books are permeated with a family sense unknown in Europe since the days of the patriarchs, by which I mean the heroic age from which the middle ages emerged, a period unable to give expression to its mode of life. *War and Peace* is an epic in which the destiny of families occupies even more space than the destinies of men. *Anna Karenina* seems an embroidering on its opening sentence about the happiness or misfortune not of men but of families. No one ever revealed, as he did, the private understanding that can exist between members of the same clan, however different in character, in mind and ability. This unity of the *gens* is somehow anterior to any individual differentiation; it exists before intellect, it precedes the person, and it persists beyond both: its existence is stronger than that of personal consciousness. In that wonderful scene in which Levin, after winning Kitty's affection, comes to ask her parents for her hand in marriage, the old prince and his wife do more than rejoice at their daughter's happiness, they literally share it. Kitty is not really separate from them; her marriage is not a personal event. In her love, in her future motherhood, she remains linked with her parents, with her ancestors, with a whole biological continuity that transcends her. It is enough to compare this scene with that between Anna and Wronski, when she has become his mistress, to realise that for Tolstoy true love, the only love that as an artist he excels in depicting, is that which is inseparable from motherhood and the family. Hence the difference of his attitude towards the love of Anna and Wronski on the one hand and that of Kitty and Levin on the other, a difference dictated by no moral prejudice but by a feeling for life more innate and deep-seated than any concern for morals.

The only love Tolstoy recognises is that which is directed to marriage and the creation of a family; a merely sensual love (like that of Natacha for Anatole in *War and Peace*), or only personal (like that of Anna), enters into his art only to reveal how such loves as these contain the seeds of death and ultimately tend to non-existence. But such a sense of the family, colouring all love, penetrating to its most secret depths and offering no hope of other "sublimation", is not by any means peculiar to Tolstoy. As a more or less unconscious instinct it belongs to all Russia. Tolstoy expressed it with unequalled power; but it is also to be found, in some degree attenuated, in Pushkin and Aksakov, in Turgenev, even in Dostoevski (though *personally* he might be a stranger to it). Even Rozanov's worship of sex never separates sexual life from procreation, and is therefore wholly different from that of a writer like

D. H. Lawrence, whose exaltation of sexual life is not altogether incompatible with contraception.

It is this close association of the erotic with family life, this fidelity of the family to its natural pre-human origins, that chiefly distinguishes Russia from the West. The family remains, even now, a powerful institution in many western countries, particularly in France; but there it is precisely as an *institution* that it commands respect and receives the protection of the law. It is something not so much given as required. A French family is founded as a new social cell, detached—one might even say severed—from the rest of society, and its members are so many citizens of a miniature State, the life of which is regulated by a constitution, an unwritten constitution but one well known to all. It is based on law rather than on morals, and on morals very much more than on primitive instinct anterior to reason. It has all the solidity of a well-built house, but not the elasticity, the power of self-renewal, that organic tissue possesses; whereas in Russia the principle of the family is organic, something vital —animal, if you will; it transcends the bounds of what is strictly the family and those of consanguinity in the more exact sense. In France, and to some extent throughout the western world, the family may be thought of in terms of common law; but in Russia, common law itself has always tended to be superseded by human relations made in the image of the family. The family was never a self-enclosed unit; it expanded, gathered to its bosom those who were strangers to it by birth: servants, guests, often a whole group of friends and "relations" were allowed to share in its private life. Such a notion as that of a "lackey", imported (like the word itself) from abroad, with the feeling of contempt that came to be associated with it, is entirely strange to Russian ideas; so much so, indeed, that all kinds of poor relations and pensioners, former midwives and wet-nurses, retired children's maids and servants of all sorts whose working years were over, formed at all times, for the Russian family, a kind of frontier guard, the implied mission of which was to defend the family against all in the outer world that was too hard, too rigid and too unhomely.

Nor was it always this extension of the real family that was the basis of feelings in all respects similar to the family feeling. These could arise in any social group that was not too large; for in Russia, more than in the West, a person remained tied to his natural environment, to what it might be better to call the community than the society, or in German terminology[1] rather *Gemeinschaft* than *Gesellschaft*. This was in the mind of Victor Hehn when he said that in Russia "the person is merged in the essence of the family"; but he made the typical mistake of confusing this feature with patriarchalism in the strict sense, whereas the *patria potestas* with its suggestion of Roman Law— the idea of the State in the bosom of the family—remains wholly alien to Russian ideas.

Jacques Rivière, in his book on *The German*, tells of the strange impression made on him by the Russian prisoners of war whom he encountered in the course of his captivity in Germany; and the thing that struck him most was precisely this lack of differentiation, proved by the way they all stuck together, one might almost say *clung* together. In the 1914 war, a group of soldiers belonging to the imperial army were admitted to an asylum in Italy suffering from a peculiar collective mental disorder. In some degree it may well be connected with this particular feature of the Russian mentality. The group obeyed implicitly a particular leader, who seemed to have concentrated in himself all the mental faculties of the rest, all their will and understanding, leaving them with nothing but a single collective soul. The case may be explained as a morbid exaggeration of that lack of personality that remained embedded in the family, in the corporation or rural community, something not to be attributed to mere "herd instinct". Every crowd or mass behaves, in certain circumstances, like a herd; but the feature of this particular mentality, so prevalent among the Russian people, is the constant feeling of being bound in close communion with those "near" to them, whether as members of the same family or clan or social group, or (at certain propitious moments) with all whom they consider to be part of themselves.

---

[1] That of Tönnies.

FEAR OF LAW

This general consideration of the family nexus leads us to another profoundly Russian characteristic: the way natural and spontaneous relations between beings take precedence over those that derive from some profession, from the place held in society, from objective and (so to speak) official rules of conduct. "A Russian business man," remarked Hehn, "is reluctant to pay a bill, even if he is a millionaire. He finds it hard to part with money and hates the idea of a precise date for having to pay. He prefers to arrange the matter amicably, in an atmosphere of friendly discussion, by way of claim and reproach, by way of promises and flattery and an appeal to the emotions, by the provisional refusal and the extorted concession, in a word on the plane of personal relations." This observation is remarkably true; but the result is not, as Hehn thought, entirely negative. More than anyone else, the Russian has always had a dread of the mechanical, of order imposed from without, of all excessive regulation of human relationships. For proof of this one has only to read Gogol's *Cloak* (1842), or the description of a government office in Goncharov's *Trivial Tale* (1847): that horrible machine which "works uninterruptedly, never taking rest, as though instead of human beings it contained nothing but wheels and springs." In the "official", however rightly or wrongly, the Russian has always looked first for the man; finding no trace of him, he has been driven to feelings of despair and indignation. When Anna Karenina begins to despise her husband she calls him a "ministerial machine"; and if Tolstoy hated him too, it was because he had conceived him as a Petersburg official: zealous, methodical, and *for that very reason* bereft of a soul. It was just this official coldness that was attributed to the capital by the inhabitants of Moscow and the provinces, who as a general rule had never much love for it. In Russian literature, a civil servant (a *chinovnik*) is almost without exception either pitiful or odious. Tolstoy had a horror of judges, Saltykov loathed all connected with the administration, Chekhov had no sympathy with professional men— except those who despised their profession. The Russian terrorists, in the main, were virtuous youths, but they held any man in uniform to be excluded automatically from the ranks of humanity: to kill him was no murder.

The Russian's anarchical instinct is not due, as might be thought, to an unbridled desire for individual freedom; quite the opposite. It comes from the fact that he is accustomed to a collective way of life in which relations between members of a group are less clearly defined and regulated, more warm and homely than would be possible in a modern State. To the same cause is due his comparative indifference to the sense of property. A German who lived in Russia before the revolution formed a highly favourable opinion of the people, but he admitted they were *diebisch angelegt*, or in other words inclined to steal. The same judgment was passed on them by Jules Legras, who remarks, however, that if the Russian is quick to purloin other people's goods he is also very ready to deprive himself of his own: it comes as natural to give away what belongs to himself as to take what belongs to another. Finding it hard to distinguish his own property from other people's, he is no better at distinguishing ownership from simple possession, or this from the more restricted enjoyment of usufruct: in most cases all he wants is the use of a thing, without laying claim to complete possession. These distinctions, that Roman Law came to impress so deeply on western peoples, especially those of the Latin civilisation, have never had much importance, outside law-courts, in Russia. As a general rule, a debt between friends never greatly disturbs the conscience of a Russian and (what is still more typical) he tends to regard every debt as such. Accordingly, when he himself lends, he never distinguishes his act very clearly from one of giving; indeed the last verb is commonly used in circumstances where in the West ambiguity would be avoided by using the verb "to lend" (*prêter*, *leihen*). One might even say that the moral consciousness of a Russian is inclined to judge all relations concerned with *having* in their purely personal aspect only. It censures, for example, an offence against the rules of property merely in so far as it is prejudicial to a person, and it would readily exculpate a thief on the ground of his poverty, or even on the ground of his victim's wealth! This peculiarity did not escape Hehn, who regarded it as something particularly odious; it is certainly fraught with great dangers and is at any rate incompatible with the logic of Roman Law, or of any law at all.

Legal logic is opposed to the intellectual consciousness of a Russian no less than it is to his moral consciousness. For him, the boundaries often disappear between what actually is and what he would like it to be, between the promise and its accomplishment, supposition and statement. The western man too may lie and steal on occasion; but when he does so it is almost always deliberately, for the sake of a very precise advantage to himself; whereas the Russian is easily tempted by the very fluidity and vagueness of what he understands by property and truth. There are two Russian words that correspond roughly to the idea of "truth"; but one of them, *istina*, implies a dignity that virtually excludes it from use in everyday life, and the other, *pravda*, means not so much the exact conformity of an x with a y as an intermediate virtue between goodness and wisdom. The Russian language itself lacks the conceptual precision that is possessed, for instance, by French; it is even phonetically inexact, so that the lack of clear articulation is what hampers a Russian most when he comes to learn French. Synonyms differ more by irrational and poetical shades of meaning than by divergencies of sense that can be exactly defined, and the conjugation of a verb, with its complicated and fleeting "aspects", has nothing in common with the rigorous distinction of tenses to be found in western languages. But, to compensate for this, Russian has something more concrete, something warmer and more sincere; one might say it is closer to things and emotions, singularly well-fitted to express *feelings* the more vividly through the very absence of the abstract and rational elements.

Nothing is more exasperating to a man from the West, when he comes in contact with a Russian, than this depreciation of law and logic in the name of something that may be above them, but may equally be beneath them; the habit of substituting for justice, and even for all judgment, a kind of resigned indulgence for human frailty, whether his own or that of others. Hehn describes how a German doctor was unable to trace anything wrong with a village sexton, the father of a large family and a notorious drunkard, and adds with great indignation that the doctor's diagnosis, though perfectly correct, aroused general resentment, on the grounds that the drunkard's children had nothing to eat and their father's supposed illness had provided them hitherto with relief from the community that kept them alive. On which side, then, were justice and truth to be found? Probably, even to-day, most Russians would prefer the doctor to lie and the hungry children get their food. "The heart has reasons," and it is not only reason that ignores them; but they are reasons unrecognised by the kind of morality that imposes prohibitions and promulgates laws. It is obvious enough that if these reasons of the heart are to prevail over morals allied to reason the result may be a chaos in which mercy and justice may perish simultaneously. But as long as this failed to occur, Russia had an advantage over the West in preserving a moral atmosphere that was more intimate and more fraternal, less chilled by the principle: "Each for himself and God for all!" This provided a strange sort of security, not so much against injustice as against an excess of justice; and it was due to the certainty that every act of the individual would be judged by his neighbours (as the Russians say) "humanly", according to the general opinion that was held of him as a human being, not as the act itself might conform (or not) to law or custom or propriety, to the categorical imperative, or to any other rule imposed from without on the man's own conscience or on that of those like him. All this has nothing to do with the *Rights of Man*, but it is not unrelated to the spirit of charity and compassion and to a certain general love for humanity.

HATRED OF FORMS

It is not only in the sphere of morals that fixity of form, the idea of rule and sanction, conflicts with the Russian's fundamental desires. If he has one phobia that is peculiar to himself, manifested as much in his everyday life and in the highest creations of his genius, it is just that of form. This he is always tempted to regard as a mask, as a showy veil that can only deceive us concerning the actual nature of the thing it envelops. No people is less attracted by the surface of things, or more willing to accept them crude, in order to be sure there is no deception. Every form is suspect, as an affectation and a reticence: it exhibits a lie while it conceals a truth. The only tolerable forms are those it is impossible to forgo, or those that are assumed by force of habit, like an old coat that no longer improves our appearance but is comfortable to wear. It is always with a shade of irony that a Russian attributes to anyone "a fine presence", and he is always keenly annoyed by the word "correct". Marked reserve suggests to him at once the idea of coldness, and he will find it hard to admit that impeccable politeness can go with true cordiality. If he had his way, every kind of formality would be banished from social relations: a man should never be conscious of playing a part. Nothing could be less Russian than Diderot's *Paradoxe sur le comédien*, for even the actor's task in Russia is not to play a part but live it on the stage.

All this is more than a simple hatred of hypocrisy; it is rather an instinctive feeling that every form as such is a species of hypocrisy, and not only this but wholly pointless and embarrassing. The largeness of soul on which a Russian prides himself (Dostoevski found it excessive, and proclaimed on one occasion his desire to restrict it) gives him a feeling of being cramped when he is compelled to depend on rule or law. This applies to grammar as much as to morals. The statesman Stolypin, when his attention was called to a solecism in one of his speeches to parliament, retorted somewhat haughtily: "Russian is my own tongue: I do what I like with it." Such an attitude, inevitably, had the effect of delaying the language from becoming fixed and prevented its being stabilised, at any rate completely, in forms amenable to definite control. It is only since the eighteenth century that Russia has possessed a literary language and in a number of respects it remains fluid to-day, even to the way certain words are pronounced. In the construction of sentences, as in the conjugation of verbs, there is a lack of logical discipline that results, incidentally, in a suppleness and freedom of expression surpassing anything at the disposal of the western languages. Its words seek to express not so much factual relations as the speaker's intention: they are oftener symbols than signs. This is why prose, in Russia, is less developed and less well used than poetical speech, and why the prose of reasoning has attained less perfection than imaginative prose.

Pushkin, in 1824, complained of Russia's lack of a "metaphysical language", namely an abstract prose; and the next hundred years, rich as they were, never succeeded completely in reversing his contention. Russian literature has excelled in poetry and fiction; it can show no equivalent to Montaigne or Pascal, to Montesquieu or Chateaubriand, in respect of the place these occupy in the literature of France. Dostoevski, its greatest thinker, expressed himself only in myths and parables. Soloviev, its greatest professional philosopher, wrote in dialogue form his last, most significant work. Later Rozanov gave his best in the guise of short familiar notes, entirely disconnected and worded with a deliberate casualness of style that is not to be matched in any literature at all; never has any great writer appeared before his public in a dress of such studied informality. As for the novelists, their language, like Tolstoy's, is deliberately rugged and uncouth; intentionally flat, like Chekhov's; or based very closely on the inflections of the spoken tongue, like Leskov's, in our own time Remizov's, or even Dostoevski's, whose genius could raise to poetry the speech of petty functionaries and even endow it with metaphysical value. It is true that Turgenev and Bunin, as the artists they were, aimed deliberately at grace and splendour of language, and the prose of Gogol, Biely, and again Remizov, has a violent expressiveness that is not always achieved without purple passages; but the actual words they all use have a living, concrete and immediate character that excuses, as it were, the skill and deliberation with which they are arranged on the page. The only perfection that is permitted and admired in Russia is that which is attributable to life itself.

Such perfection, to a Russian, is embodied for all time in the work of Pushkin: a miracle of living form, of art without artifice. But a miracle is not repeated, and in the matter of forms and life every culture, sooner or later, is confronted with the same impossibility: that of establishing between them a permanent *modus vivendi*. Either forms grow dry and shrivelled, threatening to stifle life, or else life escapes, submerging and eventually destroying all forms. After Pushkin, it was the latter that occurred. Hatred of form reached its peak in the years that saw the birth of the masterpieces of Tolstoy and Dostoevski; moreover, since it was never confined to the domain of letters, we see the same thing, after Glinka, no less markedly in music.

The musical grammar of the West, employed by Glinka with masterly ease, always repelled his successors, who regarded it as a constraint to be got rid of at all costs. Mussorgski and Tchaikovski, the most Russian of Russian musicians, succeeded in doing so by opposite methods: Mussorgski by revolting against it directly (incidentally without ever having thoroughly understood it), Tchaikovski by yielding to it, but not accepting it completely or adopting it for his own; so that emotion, with him, instead of being embodied in form, overflows it and renders it somehow insignificant. As for the plastic arts, they were distinguished in the eighteenth century from the art of the West (which they then followed closely) by a certain lack of strictness, an often gracious freedom in design and construction. It is by an element of softness, a lack of tension, that the sculptured portraits of Chubin, or the painted portraits of Levitski, differed from the French works of their day (peculiarities, incidentally, that one is tempted sometimes to attribute simply to the typically Russian features of their sitters). In the next century, the same softness is found in the works of artists like Venetsianov and Fedotov, and even in the otherwise so vigorous Surikov. Not only so, but the empire-style architecture, especially in Moscow and the provinces, did its utmost to free itself from classical rigour. In spite of superficial likenesses, there is nothing so contrary to the spirit of a French-designed building of the time of Napoleon as the house of a Russian country-gentleman, in the midst of fields or woodlands, with its shy entablature and pasty columns, the long retreating line of its single storey and the familiar samovar steaming in the porch.

It is no great help to the artist, this distrust of forms and desire to neutralise them, and Russian art in the last century suffered much from its fear of art. Lack of any faith in painting, as such, led painters to be careless of pictorial processes and to apply them haphazard, in the fallacious hope that "soul" and "feeling" would prevail over every difficulty and largely compensate for other shortcomings. In the same sort of way, a poet like Nekrassov was so impatient of formal discipline, so afraid of passing for an artist, that in spite of his great gifts he habitually made use of the most outworn clichés. Form took vengeance by delivering him over to the wooliest forms of expression. Yet all the great works produced by Russia in the last century owe their principal merits to this very same instinct. Thus Tolstoy's absurd theoretical invectives against Shakespeare or Wagner—against all art as such and all poetry as such—are only the reverse side of the medal of which the obverse side is his own creative genius. In the same way western admirers of Chekhov are often admiring, without knowing it, just Russian life itself: the life that in his stories he allows to speak for itself, with a personal self-effacement that is the negation of all that is commonly called art, though it is, in fact, simply his own particular art. The sincerity and spontaneity, the intensity and verve and freshness of emotion, all the qualities most admired in what is known of Russian works in the West, necessarily presuppose this defiance of form by those who have least hope of ever doing without it. And even if this defiance had only negative results we could never regard it as simply an incidental weakness, a mere aberration: it has far deeper roots, religious in character, in all that is most intimate in the Russian soul.

THE SPIRIT OF HUMILITY

The key to this revolt against form is provided by the fact that ancient Russia knew nothing of it. Her ikon painters, her architects and preachers, never feared to aspire to formal perfection: in beauty, as they saw it, there was nothing scandalous. But the reason was, that they were never expected to conceive it except in its natural context; it remained in their eyes what it had always been, a reflection of the divine glory. It was only the laicised Russia of the last two centuries that was confronted with a beauty that had descended to the earth, a beauty separate from other attributes of divinity and distinct from all celestial beatitude. There is no clearer sign of the persistence in the Russian soul of the need for religion than its deliberate refusal of this new state of affairs. For the hatred of forms, just as the fear of law, is ultimately nothing else but the refusal to recognise any value at all in complete isolation, wrenched from the unity of all values in God.

We have seen already how love of truth and aspiration after the good retain a symbolical union in the Russian word *pravda*. In the same way the distrust of science as such, so often manifested by Russians—of science, that is, without concern for anything else—and even their distrust of the crude utilitarianism to which they have rallied at various times, can only be explained by their unconscious and no doubt naïve desire to attain, all at once, this sudden transcendence of truth, when it will be no longer distinguishable from supreme moral value. Similarly in Old Slav, the language of the Russian Church, the word *dobrota* combines the meaning of beauty and goodness: a beauty that is good, goodness that is beautiful; in comparison with this, the good by itself would appear merely insipid and beauty by itself a dangerous abstraction. Anything beautiful in art, suspected of not being also good and true, inspires a Russian, whether he is an artist or not, with a feeling somewhat akin to shame: it is a mere flower of rhetoric, an empty decoration, a confession of vanity. "Don't speak prettily" (that is, elegantly, and *therefore*, to some extent, emptily): Turgenev puts these words in the mouth of his nihilist in *Fathers and Sons*; but he might have attributed them equally well to any of the greatest of his country's poets. Admittedly it is not necessary to be a Russian to prize simplicity before all else, to value justice of tone, lack of emphasis and soberness in the choice of means; for this it is enough to have classical taste. But in Pushkin, indeed, it is due to something more than taste. Pushkin desired to remain simple because he desired to be true; he disdained ornament more and more because he declined to cast a veil over the humble nakedness of the human state.

Genius, in his case, enabled him to avoid the rocks that were fraught with so much danger, as we have seen, to other artists. Of these a single example is enough. Alexander Ivanov, far the ablest Russian painter in modern times, was half embarrassed by his own talent, distrusted his direct vision of things, and chose to work on a vast canvas for thirty years on end: it was *The Apparition of Christ to the People*, and he finally spoilt it through too much reading of the manuals of archæology and David Strauss, through trying to make it too truthful, with a too obvious moral purpose.

Values, once separated, are not easily reunited in any new synthesis, yet it was of such a synthesis, all unconsciously, that the Russian geniuses of the last century were always dreaming. As long as unity is still something to be sought for, it must be free at any rate from all idolatry: there must be no affectation, but an unmasking of human pride. The Christianity that imbued the Russian people so deeply made them suspicious of human greatness, which they regarded as a kind of statue in search of its own pedestal. A great personal feat, even performed in a great cause, would strike them as something false; a great sentence, however full of meaning, had an empty look if it was too well turned. To Tolstoy, Napoleon was only another William II; Shakespeare meant nothing to him because the imagery of his language and his dramatic conventions were tantamount to lies. The versified eloquence of Victor Hugo has always been baffling to Russian readers, for whom even Baudelaire, in some places, was too rhetorical for their tastes. It is perhaps true in a certain sense, as Weininger held, that the Russians are of all peoples the least Greek in temperament. They would certainly have been pleased by the ugliness of Socrates, but they would have found Demosthenes too garrulous, Alcibiades too handsome, Pericles too brilliant and Plato too wise. It is impossible, at any rate, to imagine a Russian tragedy, whether real or imaginary, acted in buskins and masks. Even in our own day the master of Soviet Eurasia takes care to avoid all impressive postures and the vocal achievements of his late western rivals.

A certain effacement of personality, if only exterior, seems a thing both natural and desirable to a Russian. Often such an effacement is partly involuntary; in so far, that is, as the human person is merged, to some extent, in the collective life of the family or community. But it is primarily something demanded for religious reasons—even if they are no longer recognised as such—and by religious we mean Christian. Self-assertion, to the Russian—assertion of personal rights, and still more the will to power—is either wholly strange or else something he encounters in devious ways, shunning the light of day. Egotism as a theory is repulsive to his nature, and if he himself behaves selfishly (as he may, like everyone else) it is not his way to feel pride in so doing. He often seems deficient, to western eyes, of a sense of personal dignity; but it would be fairer to say he has a different idea of it, one that doesn't constrain him to appear affluent when he is poor, or to be ashamed of either his infirmities or his misfortunes. He is perfectly capable, as his literature shows, of admiring the quality of buoyancy in a character, but he is apt to appreciate it better in someone other than himself. Woman, in the course of the last century, won her important position in Russian life, not by fighting for it, as she did in the Anglo-Saxon countries, but as a result of man's coming to see her, more than elsewhere, as a human person equal in value to himself, rather than as a mere instrument of pleasure or an object of utility. The cult of force and the strong man never went further in Russia than its purely infantile and harmless stage; and Rozanov, though he simplified matters, was not very far wrong. "Nietzsche," he wrote, "is cried up because he is a German and because he is a sick man. But if a Russian, speaking for himself, had uttered such an aphorism as this: 'If you see a man falling, give him a push,' he would have been regarded as nothing more nor less than a blackguard, and no one would have dared to be seen reading him."

The spirit of charity and humility—this is the best thing the Russians have retained from all their nine centuries of Christian education; and what, if not that, is the essence of the Gospel? Indeed Russia has allowed herself to be so imbued with the New Testament that she has tended to neglect the preliminary training of the Old; she has listened so well to the Sermon on the Mount that she has come to make little of the Ten Commandments. That, no doubt, is why she has no sense of law and legal procedure, why she distrusts any morality that has a resemblance to law. Anything like a system or rule is a departure from the human—and also from the divine. Russian Orthodoxy's old objection to Catholicism is just that juridical spirit which seems inseparable from the doctrine and organisation of the Roman Church. Charity and compassion, in Russian eyes, not only transcend justice: they tend to abolish it altogether and render it superfluous.

Such a view as this, applied to practical conduct, ends inevitably in rejecting what the West esteems highest: moral obligation and the sense of duty. If a Russian does good it is nine times out of ten out of love that he does it: out of sympathy, out of his instinct for charity, even out of caprice; but never out of duty. Even if it is simply a matter of work, he never performs it satisfactorily unless his heart happens to be in it; never if he is obliged—whatever the character of the obligation. If he does perform his duty, he more or less resents it; and this remains true of a duty to himself, one that he clearly understands is for his own future benefit. Such an attitude may easily degenerate into passivity, into simple laziness, into *sinful* laziness. Yet Goncharov was not entirely wrong, while praising the merits and energy of Stolz, to have a sneaking preference for the indolent Oblomov, who came to grief through his incapacity to act; certainly Russian readers would all have shared this preference, remembering Stolz was a German whose name meant "pride". The denial of duty, the deducing of all morality from a spontaneous love of one's neighbour, the setting of charity above any kind of justice—all this is dangerous; but it is not without beauty and not far removed from the spirit of the Gospel. It implies faith in a principle of good that is at once positive and active; whereas morality of the western sort can so easily degenerate into a system of prohibitions, into an idea of the good that can be reduced to a mere abstention from evil, exalting obedience to an abstract principle and finally desiccating even the noblest of souls. Pharisaism is not a distinctive failing of the Russian: his sins are the publican's.

Charity, as long as it remains Christian, cannot be separated from the spirit of humility. It is here we approach what is most precious and deep-hidden in the spiritual life of the Russian people. Jacques Rivière must have been aware of it, after hearing *Boris Godunov*, when he wrote: "Mussorgski's melody is the tale of humility." And he added: "Humility—not a negative feeling, a mere constraint of pride—but something very much alive, lovely to behold, at once shy and intrepid . . ." So far from being a constraint to the Russian soul, it is its vehicle for expressing its most natural impulse and its profoundest intuition: that of God's own infinite capacity for self-abasement.[1] This impulse and intuition are not, it is true, the monopoly of any one people or of any particular section of Christendom: they belong to the life of the Universal church. They were already there in the age of the Apostles, and they can never be wholly absent from Christian faith and Christian consciousness. In the domain of art, no one, not even Dostoevski, has expressed them better and with deeper understanding that did that great religious genius, Rembrandt. And without going so far back we can find them in that wonderful second scene of the second act of Claudel's *Hostage*, in which the priest Badilon says to Sygne de Coûfontaine:

> *God is not above us but below.*
> *It is according to your weakness, not your strength, I tempt you.*

If there is a peculiarly Russian sound in these two lines of the great Catholic poet, it is because Christianity is one; but it is also because no Christian people has chosen, as have the Russians, for the central theme of their meditation and piety, this God who is beneath us, who tries us not for our strength but for our weakness. Already in old Russia, this theme and shade of feeling had prevailed in the lives of its saints and in its religious poetry, and the same influence is traceable in the old ikon painting. Derjavin, at the end of the eighteenth century, was the last of the poets in modern Russia to have a glimpse of

---

[1] In theological language this humiliation of God, manifested in the Incarnation and in the Passion of Jesus Christ, is expressed by the Greek term *kenosis*.

God enthroned in majesty. Since then no one gazed heavenward to see him: men have looked for him below, in the suffering of their neighbours, in the misery and forsakenness of their own hearts. Dostoevski saw an image of the Blessed Virgin in the motherhood of the lowly earth itself, and all his creations are inwardly sustained by a central intuition which is one of humility, of the humiliation of Jesus Christ. The whole Russian literature of the last century, all that derived from the *Postmaster* of Pushkin rather than Gogol's *Cloak*, turns on this same intuition, opening up for every writer new creative perspectives, though the particular writer may have been anything but a believer, or actually a professed enemy of the Christian faith. Even some of the revolutionaries, some of the *fin-de-siècle* terrorists, were imbued in their own fashion with this very same spirit, the only thing then in common between the culture of the élite and the moral life of the people. Everything, as we have seen, is linked together with this—the hatred of pharisaism and rhetorical elaboration, the distrust of outward display, the love of that beauty which is one with the good—everything, in fact, that is most Russian in the Russian soul.

THE FATAL ANTITHESIS

Russia in the eyes of the West, as in those of its own "westernisers", has had the appearance in every age of a backward country, in many respects primitive; on the face of things, the leading characteristics of its interior life would seem to be far from contradicting this opinion. What is false in it is due simply to the criterion of value that has usually accompanied it. To anyone, considering modern civilisation, who would not give first priority to its urban, technical and rationalist aspects, an archaic culture need not necessarily be inferior. Hehn himself, with all the disgust he felt for Russia as a whole, was by no means insensible to its peculiar charms: youth and spaciousness, inexhaustible possibilities, an absence of water-tight compartments and too-restricting boundaries. In Russia, at any rate in the Russia of the old régime, there was something that is only a memory in the West: freedom of movement, facilities to do what one wanted, a stressing of the future rather than the past, things scarcely known in more "advanced" countries, living a life more differentiated, more subject at every turn to painful calculation. It may well be argued that the hold taken on the West by Russian literature and art was due purely and simply to their happy backwardness, compared with forms of art that were doubtless more sophisticated, but drier, more intellectualised, in danger sometimes of a kind of sclerosis. And when people spoke of the primitiveness of "holy Russia", surely what they meant, very often, was that Russia had remained imbued with Christian ideas, as was not the case any longer, not in the same way or to the same degree, with the other countries of Europe.

Having said so much, we must admit that the condition of Russian culture, in its relations to the civilisation of the West, was not free from dangers to Russia herself. In so far as it was a matter of no more than deficiencies in her technical or industrial equipment, it was relatively easy to face the problem and make up lost time in comparatively few years. But in all that concerned more intimate obstacles, the struggle to surmount them involved far greater strain. It might even be doubted if there was any real will to engage in the struggle. If Russia, after living a thousand years, could preserve characteristics like those we have described as family connection, fear of law and hatred of forms, it was because she had constantly opposed a kind of passive resistance to what history demanded of her. In so far as it had been possible, she had always yielded to the pressure of events, forgoing the attempt to master them by any organised and continuous effort. If she had been asked her opinion, in any period of her development, she would have preferred the least possible tension and constraint, she would have chosen a peaceful and rather sleepy existence rather than the stern necessities that a *historical* life imposes upon nations. Generally speaking, she seems to be whispering the strange aspiration contained in those words of Rozanov, words that only a Russian could have written: "I am like a child in its mother's womb, reluctant to be born. I am warm enough here."

Russia's predilection, it is true, for the pre-natal state did not prevent her from being imbued with the Christian faith; but here again—and this touches the decisive problem of her destiny—the elements of that faith which she decided to choose were the purest, the most human, and also the most superhuman; but they were also those least susceptible of being used for worldly ends. In the religious life of the Orthodox Christian the accent is less on Christ's Nativity and Passion than on his Resurrection, less on obstacles to be overcome and a course to be run than on the willing renunciation of the goods of this world with a view to beatitude in heaven. Humility and charity are undoubtedly the elements that are most Christian in Christian ethics, but for building the city of God *on earth* other virtues besides these are required: virtues, the cynic would say, more amenable to compromise. It is not easy to regard as types of Christianity unalloyed, the knight, the courtier and the *honnête homme*; least of all that most potent figure of all, the "gentleman"; yet in the history of the various countries that have produced them, the constructive part taken by all these types has been one of enormous importance. In Russia, on the other hand, the holy old man, the life-long pilgrim, the fool for the love of God, though entering much more directly into the spirit of the Gospel, have never counted for much in their own country's history. This acquiescence in doing nothing when it is impossible to do all, this contempt for any good that is not the supreme good, has been a source of greatness for Russia but also a cause of her downfall.

For historical necessities remain; a refusal to have dealings with them must result, sooner or later, in having to submit to them. The real danger for Russia came not from anything primitive; it came from what was amorphous in her. Feudal society, primitive though it may seem in modern eyes, created an elaborate structure based on a complex of hierarchies; it was this structure, we have seen, that was chiefly lacking in Russia. Truly enough, all manner of hierarchies were imposed on her from above, and also from without; but all she did was to submit to them. She never believed in them; which means she inwardly rejected them—the natural with the artificial, the true with the false. The Russians know how to respect suffering and misery—better, no doubt, than any other Christian people; they know how to love the poor, and even the poor in spirit, without the deviating of such love into simple pity, without its ever being stained with a tinge of condescension. But what they do not know is respect for personal worth and ability, for the virtues of creation and command; least of all can they accept authority, however freely recognised and founded on merit. Physical force has seemed preferable to spiritual authority, for it required no assent and was content with mere obedience. They could resign themselves to obey; they would accept injustice out of fear of justice; in their desire to avoid all rule they would allow themselves to be subjected to the hardest of all rules. It was thus there arose and became established the fatal antithesis to everything we have observed up to now, the tragic negation of all that has been dearest to the Russian soul.

After being too complacent with lack of form, to have to submit to an excess of it was only to be expected. In art, there was Gogol's failure, when he sought to impose on his *Dead Souls* an artificial construction based on Dante's *Divine Comedy*. Nearer to us than this, we have had the formalist casuistry of Brussov, a reaction against the total absence of form in the poets of the previous generation. In the social and political sphere, the consequences of a similar attitude were far more serious. Victor Hehn was the first to draw attention to this; he noted the violent discrepancy between the secret leaning and the apparent reality, detesting both, as he did, with equal fervour. Never tired of abusing Russia for her lack of personal differentiation, for the fact that "the Russian's moral world begins and ends with the family", he proclaims, nevertheless, the Russian's peculiar reverence for "order, in the mechanical sense of the word". "Nowhere else," he observes, "is there such an abstract and mechanical attitude to any task, as if culture all depended on rules and formulas imposed by decree." These words sound prophetic, but they could find their illustrations in the past just as well. It was when family connections and amorphous fraternities passed away that they were always replaced in Russia by their antitheses, which were nothing but the result of their own excesses: such was the reign of the mechanised State and the barracks, of dreary administrative regulation, all that horrified the contemporaries of Peter the Great, all that caused Nicholas I to be hated, all that appears to-day in the most odious aspects of the knouto-soviet Empire. The contrast, here, is not between the citizen's freedom and an autocratic régime, but between the State at its hardest and man at his most fluid, between a soulless political machine and a naked soul in isolation, without form or bounds —what the Russian people had always prized above all.

The antinomy goes to the depths of Russian history and Russian life. Every attempt at construction in Russia has been made *against* Russia and has provoked her resistance—her own sort of resistance. The State, the Empire, the men of St. Petersburg—these were always like Tolstoy's Karenin, who sets out from Moscow fairly bristling with clear and aggressive intentions, then suddenly grows limp and soft and uncertain, losing, as it were, his moral backbone, as soon as he encounters his brother-in-law Oblonski, the incarnation of everything in vast Russia that is amiably shapeless, all that is vaguely good-natured. In Tolstoy himself, his primary and vital instinct was in conflict with something else in him: his purely intellectual schemes, those dissertations, half historical half philosophical, which he felt bound to insert in *War and Peace*, and (still more) the rigorous moralisings of his late old age. Abstract thought, with him, tended always towards rigour, a rigour as naïve, as quasi-arithmetical, as its real rhythm was slow and spasmodic. This conflict that was waged between Tolstoy and himself is akin to that between the Russias of Oblonski and Karenin, between the soft community of souls without frontiers and its rigid encasement by a rational State. The struggle, it may be, is one without issue; ultimately it is this that has brought upon the country the sub-human régime it has endured for thirty years.

But the true Russia, for every Russian, is closer to Tolstoy's art than to his thought, to Oblonski than to Karenin. The most clear-sighted judgment she has ever inspired was found among the papers of Gogol: the author of it, Philarete, the metropolitan of Moscow. The Russian people, he remarked, has "little light, but plenty of warmth". A familiar Russian proverb censures whatever "gives light without warming", but no one ever retorts against the thing that gives warmth without light. The Russia that never desired to be born, that said, "I am warm enough here," may now be dead; or perhaps she has merely stolen out of sight and one day we shall see her again. In the testimony of her faith, her art and her thought, certainly this, and no other, is the Russia we find.